Pansies

How to Grow, Reimagine, and Create Beauty
with Pansies and Violas

BRENNA ESTRADA

PHOTOGRAPHY BY Kelly Bowie

Timber Press
Workman Publishing
Hachette Book Group, Inc.
1290 Avenue of the Americas
New York, New York 10104
timberpress.com

Timber Press is an imprint of Workman Publishing, a division of Hachette Book Group, Inc. The Timber Press name and logo are registered trademarks of Hachette Book Group, Inc.

Printed in China on responsibly sourced paper

Text design by Ashley Martinez Lima
Cover design by Hillary Caudle

The publisher is not responsible for websites (or their content) that are not owned by the publisher.

ISBN 978-1-64326-400-4

A catalog record for this book is available from the
Library of Congress.

For my beloved husband and my dear friend Meredith.
This book would not have metamorphosed from thought to ink
without their unfaltering belief and support.

Contents

Preface

This book is a heartfelt plea. Written on behalf of the pansy, and pursued in hope and optimism, it has a single purpose: to elevate the pansy to a reimagined role of elegance and secure its place in at least a few more hearts and gardens for some years to come.

Pansies have not always been my favorite. I saw them quite differently when I was a child. To be honest, I didn't really see them at all—or at least not as I do now. They were always just there: down low, beneath the shrubs, filling pots, on racks at the hardware store, and in unkept flower beds throughout my hometown. And they were always in just three colors, red, yellow, and purple. Pansies seemed so common to me then. I was not yet aware that they held secrets, or that there were centuries of history behind the little blossoms with the signature dark blotch. My love of pansies did not begin until many years later when an esteemed grower and mentor I was working for at the time introduced me to an entirely different side of this ubiquitous flower.

The pansies and violas that awakened my passion were not red, yellow, or purple. They were a multitude of hues in between, with markings and textures that I had never before seen in a pansy, or any other flower. They ranged from burgundy, vermilion, and mauve to terra-cotta, bronze, and antiqued gold. There were shades of pale blush, smoky apricot, and creamy lemon yellow, and the colors were spread across the petals in splashes, streaks, and tiny rivers, with intricate veining and penciling. Some were striped like fierce little tigers watching you from within the garden walls, while others were ruffled and flounced, determined to be seen. It wasn't until their beauty lured me in for a closer look that I realized the air around them was permeated with a scent reminiscent of chocolate. I had been unaware of the intoxicating fragrance some pansies and violas possess. And that was it. The path before me shifted dramatically, and I was embarking on a deliciously aromatic, velvet-lined journey into past centuries with a heartfelt determination to preserve the future of these tenacious little flowers.

After being nudged down the pansy rabbit hole, my curiosity became insatiable. Every time I found an answer, it prompted further questions. I bought every book I could find that spoke of the pansy, including countless old garden books with snippets of text referencing their curious past. Nearly all the books I gathered were published within an eighty-year span, from the 1830s to the 1910s. While a few additional books were written throughout the 1900s, I was able to find only two that were truly substantial. They were published in 1958 and 1990 by authors who, like myself, were passionate about these little flowers and felt the need to speak up on their behalf. I further scoured articles and interviews, searching archival logs of former pansy societies and historical online libraries. I visited antiquarian booksellers in the United Kingdom, ordered volumes from small shops in Europe, and received calls from kind booksellers in Canada happy to discuss the condition of a particular volume's illustrated plates. I had to know why there was such a sudden end to the frenzied craze that had surrounded the pansy for decades. I also needed to know how to bring it the recognition and attention it so very much deserves today.

The hours I was not engrossed in literary searches and studies were spent in my garden, documenting the thousands of pansies and violas I was growing throughout my years of trials. I aimed to learn which were the most beautiful and unique, which were the most fragrant, which could be grown for cut flowers, and which would bloom in the heat of summer and the cold of winter. I was not trialing them as a nursery or breeder would, but rather as an enthusiast and a small-scale flower farmer, so my standards and measures of success were different. Because I wanted to know exactly how pansies did under average circumstances, in an average garden, grown by an average person, I did not provide them with the extreme protection or kind of care a commercial grower would. It is these flowers that you will find lovingly photographed throughout this book. Grown by me, on my little farm, on my little island, in the Pacific Northwest, and I am fully confident that you are equally capable of growing them.

I can now say that it was only by hearing about this flower from the many voices of the past that I have been able to see it for all that it is. I do not believe any other flower holds as much history, sentiment, potential, perseverance, and character as the pansy. I have done my best to fill these pages justly so you will come to believe it too.

Phosphorus.

J. Freeman del:

W. Annan lith: 12. Gracechurch St.

CHAPTER 1

The History of the Pansy and Viola

Pansy or Viola?

What is the difference between a viola and a pansy? Technically, all pansies are violas, but not all violas are pansies. Both are members of the botanical family Violaceae, and distinguishing between the two can be quite confusing and extremely difficult, if not on occasion near impossible due to centuries of cross-pollinating and hybridization. While *Viola* is Latin for the whole genus, it has also been applied to a section within that genus. If this wasn't confusing enough, the term *violetta* has been used to reference specific violas that are heavily fragrant and compact. The violas I will be referencing in this book are all within the section *Melanium*.

FAMILY: Violaceae
SUBFAMILY: Violoideae
TRIBE: Violeae
GENUS: *Viola* (pansies, violas, violettas, and violets)
SECTION: *Melanium*
SPECIES: *V. tricolor* (heartsease)
     V. cornuta
     V. lutea
      V. ×wittrockiana (garden pansy)
        (*V. tricolor* crossed with *V. lutea*)
          V. ×williamsii (viola and violetta)
            (*V. ×wittrockiana* crossed with *V. cornuta*)

Pansy 'Phosphorus' from *A History and Description of the Different Varieties of the Pansey, or Heartsease, now in Cultivation in the British Gardens*, Sinclair & Freeman, 1835.

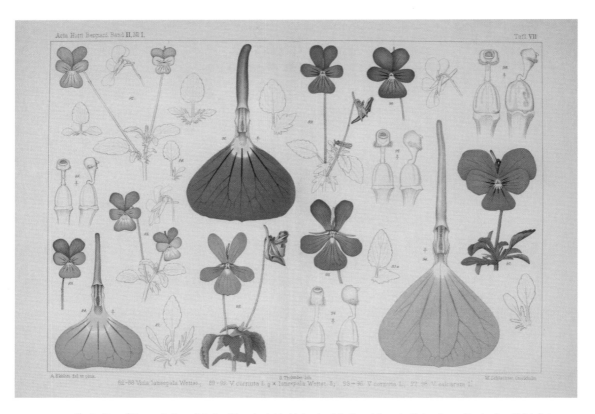

Illustration of *V. cornuta from Acta horti bergiani : Meddelanden från Kongl,* Svenska Vetenskaps-Akademiens Trädgård Bergielund, Band II, No 1, 1892.

There are currently over six hundred recognized species in the genus *Viola,* yet most of us have heard of only a few. *Viola odorata* and *V. tricolor* are the most familiar and most present in historic texts, literature, and art. *Viola odorata* (sweet violet) has long been grown and remarked on for its fragrance. Think of *My Fair Lady* and Eliza Doolittle's humble beginning as a flower seller in Covent Garden waving about a hand-tied, sweetly scented bunch of purple flowers. *Viola tricolor,* which possesses a gentler and quite different fragrance, is the *Viola* species most often referenced in poetry and prose throughout the centuries. According to one legend, the Greek god Eros loved little white pansies, so Aphrodite, the goddess of love, turned them into three colors to halt his affections. *Viola tricolor* was also known to be a favorite flower of Queen Elizabeth I. At court, paintings and other artifacts of the time show many examples of violas and pansies, including embroidery on the queen's gowns. When she was still Princess Elizabeth and just eleven years old, she even coverstitched the flowers on a prayer-book cover for Katherine Parr, the final wife of Henry VIII.

The Importance of the Past

You can't really know where you are going until you know where you have been. —MAYA ANGELOU

I believe that knowing the history will always yield a better understanding of the present and a clearer and more reliable path to the future. This can be said of people, of places, of things, even of animals, and also of flowers like the pansy and the viola. As a grower, understanding how a flower thrives in its native environment is crucial for ensuring it thrives in the environment in which you intend to grow it. It's also important to understand how it has been hybridized and what traits it has taken on, as these factors significantly affect the type of care it will need.

Animals and plants are often bred to serve a specific purpose, but as time passes and other options prove superior, it is possible for their original intent and history to be overlooked or even forgotten. A few years ago, we lost our greater Swiss mountain dog after eleven incredible years with him. The Swissy was originally bred as a working dog—"the poor man's horse," as I had heard on more than one occasion—often pulling carts laden with milk for farmers who could not afford a draft horse. We have never needed to move milk carts on our little farm, so he was simply our companion and farm protector. But the fact that his genetics allowed him to pull incredible amounts of weight was important for us to know so we could ensure his happiness and safety.

When I decided to remain within the pansy rabbit hole, digging further and further down rather than finding my way back up, I knew that understanding the past of the pansy was going to be an important part of championing its future. Pansies and violas have a long and multifaceted history. They were held in high esteem within art and literature, having been given the reputation in folklore of being a key ingredient in love potions. They were also considered a highly sentimental flower and were incorporated into décor and fashion for centuries, their presence bringing constant joy and remembrance. Pansies and violas have a long history in apothecary as well, and are currently making a comeback as an edible ingredient of beauty in restaurants.

While more modern ways of doing things will often render older versions obsolete, it doesn't necessarily mean those things are no longer able to serve their original purpose. I am an avid collector of antiques, furniture included. I have often found the older styles of things to be more reliable and possess superior longevity, even if they are not as fast or convenient. I prefer a manual coffee grinder, while my husband prefers an electric one. My manual grinder will last indefinitely, while I've already had to replace our electric grinder twice. I prefer to type on my 1956 Olympia SM3 typewriter rather than my MacBook. I can take it anywhere I want and type out letters or thoughts with no power or printer needed, and I won't need to replace it due to outdated software. My typewriter served its purpose for decades before I existed and will continue to serve that purpose for decades after I am gone.

When the pansy craze ended in the early twentieth century, their use as a cut flower seemed to end with it. They were further pushed aside to make room for flowers that were newly accessible as a result of progressive strides in global transport. No longer present in florist shops, their future was almost entirely relegated to bedding and borders. For decades since, they have been hybridized to be as compact as possible, suited to their resigned position beneath the shrubs. But drawings of the pansy and viola from previous centuries show a natural long-stem growth habit. By embracing this original habit, the pansy reclaims its usefulness as a cut flower. Had I not understood how the pansy naturally grew when allowed to, I could not have understood its potential as a particularly lovely cut flower.

I was further intrigued to find that in the same span of years that I had been pursuing the long forgotten potential of the pansy, there were scientists in Violaceae research actively working to update its taxonomy. Their scientific study shows the viola may actually have some origins in South America. Despite it being one of the most popular flowers of the nineteenth and twentieth centuries, there is still plenty to learn, and I am excited to see what else is uncovered.

Violas, particularly *Viola odorata*, can confidently be traced as far back as the fourth century BCE, where they were used for their medicinal benefits throughout Greece and sold for their fragrance in Athens. They have been praised by poets for just as long. They were present in the garden of Calypso on Ogygia in *The Odyssey*, written around the seventh century BCE, and their medicinal use was present throughout the Middle Ages.

In the early to mid-sixteenth century, German botanists Otto Brunfels and Leonhart Fuchs first referred to *herba trinitatis*, the medieval Latin name for *Viola tricolor*. Published between 1530 and 1536, the multivolume *Herbarum vivae eicones* by Brunfels was considered revolutionary at the time, as it went beyond just the medicinal use of flowers, and both the descriptions and illustrations (woodcuts by

Illustration from *De historia stirpium commentarii insignes*, Leonhart Fuchs, 1542.

Kreyschamkraut.　　CCCCLXI·

Hans Weiditz) of the plants were based on firsthand observation rather than ancient texts. In addition to being a botanist, Leonhart Fuchs was also a practicing physician. He took botany into a more scientific study with his book, *De historia stirpium commentarii insignes* (1542), which focused on the habitats and traits of the plants themselves, rather than simply passing along their traditional use, as had been done in centuries past. Fuchs sought out three talented artists to illustrate his book. Albrecht Meyer painted the plants from nature in watercolor, Heinrich Füllmaurer then transferred the paintings to woodblocks, after which Veit Rudolph Speckle cut and printed them. The illustration of the *V. tricolor* in Fuchs's book shows the long stems true to its original habit, a habit that has passed to many of its descendants despite ongoing hybridization efforts to make them more compact.

Around that same time, French botanist Jean Ruel (Ruellius) made mention of the pansy as *pensea* in his book *De natura stirpium* (1536), referring to it as an odorless viola. The little flower was also gaining notoriety in the Netherlands, where Rembert Dodoens (Dodonaeus) wrote about *V. tricolor* in his book *Florum, et coronariarum odoratarumque nonnullarum herbarum historia* (1568). The book contained 108 woodblock illustrations of many flowers, including *V. tricolor,* and fascinatingly, those woodblocks still exist today in a museum in Antwerp. In 1629, the renowned English botanist John Parkinson wrote of *V. tricolor* being called by many names, including *V. flammea, V. multicolor, Flos trinitatis,* and *Herba clauellata,* pointing out that the English commonly referred to it as Harts ease and pansy, from the French *pensée.*

During this time, the viola, no longer confined to the studies of botany and medicine alone, was being grown ornamentally across France, England, and the Netherlands. By the mid-seventeenth century, it had gained popularity in Italy, Denmark, Sweden, and Poland as well. Throughout the eighteenth century, the viola continued to flower true in color and habit to its origination as a wild flower, and it wasn't until the nineteenth century that extensive ornamental cultivation of it took place. While the pansy was already in cultivation from the *Viola lutea* by the seventeenth century, it also continued to hold habits and colors very close to its wild origins. As with the viola, it wasn't until the early nineteenth century that the garden pansy we know today was extensively cultivated and perfected. It first took place in England, where *V. lutea* and *V. tricolor* were growing wild in abundance at the time.

Viola tricolor, commissioned by Emperor Rudolph II, between 1596 and 1610.

flos trinitalis. faceus viola tricolor.
Penseen.

Penseen. | flos trinitalis. viola tricolor. | des pensées.

Viola tricolor.

The Origination of the Garden Pansy

These little Ladies' Delights have infinite variety of expression; some are laughing and roguish, some sharp and shrewd, some surprised, others worried, all are animated and vivacious, and a few saucy to a degree.

—ALICE MORSE EARLE, American historian and author of *Old Time Gardens* (1901)

Understanding the garden pansy requires a closer look at *Viola tricolor, V. lutea,* and *V. cornuta.*

Viola tricolor, the original heartsease, boasts two upper petals of light to deep purple and three lower petals of yellow to orange with distinct rays around the eye. It grows native in meadows, fields, hedgerows, woodlands, and sandy banks throughout Europe. It is, along with *V. lutea,* a parent plant to the garden pansy we know today.

Viola lutea, also known as the mountain pansy, is native to western and central Europe. *Lutea* is Latin for yellow, and most flowers do bloom in soft shades of yellow, though they can occasionally be purple as well. These sweet blooms prefer rocky landscapes and have a gentle creeping habit.

Viola cornuta is native to the Pyrenees regions of France and Spain, allowing it to tolerate warmer conditions better than other violas. It is often called the horned pansy or tufted pansy, and its root base grows in more of a gathered clump than the other species. This allows the plants to be divided every three or four years and grown as perennials accordingly. The horn at the back of the viola reflects its hardiness: the more pronounced the horn, the more vigorous the plant. *Viola cornuta* played a significant role in the hybridization of the viola, the pansy, and the violetta. Its superior tolerance of warm weather and perennial growing habit were key in cultivating new varieties that were both visually appealing and hardy.

Interest in *V. cornuta* increased significantly in the 1860s. A notable variety called 'Maggie Mott' was developed around this time. Silvery mauve and of exceptional fragrance, it is one of few violas from this era still available today. John Wills, who was at that time the head gardener at Oulton Park, Cheshire, and whose efforts were later noted in the July 21, 1892, edition of the *Journal of Horticulture, Cottage Gardener, and Home Farmer,* brought significant attention to the viola with his extraordinary displays. By the 1870s, careful attention was being paid to violas in cultivation throughout England and Scotland. Mr. B. S. Williams introduced 'Perfection',

Illustration from *Flora Londinensis,* 1777.

'Enchantress', and 'Magnificent', and Mr. William Dean raised a variety called 'True Blue', which was said to be the best blue viola available at that time and for many years thereafter.

In 1872, Dr. Charles Stuart of Chirnside, New Brunswick, further worked to cross *V. cornuta* with the garden pansy (*V. tricolor* and *V. lutea*). Two years later, he applied pollen from pansy 'Blue King' to *V. cornuta,* which resulted in some noteworthy new varieties, blue in flower like the pansy but with the tufted habit of the viola. They were initially called tufted pansies to separate them from the other violas and pansies currently in cultivation. He further added pollen from a pink pansy, which created additional varieties that were still tufted in habit but had a much wider range of color. He took cuttings from the best of these specimens and submitted them for show, along with sending some off to the warmer and drier climate in the south of England to see how they fared. In 1887, one of his seedlings produced a pure white, highly fragrant flower completely devoid of rays, and he took ample cuttings to ensure its longevity for further cultivation.

While Dr. Stuart considered himself just a "humble amateur," he had succeeded in developing a perennial pansy of tufted habit that proved exceptional in the garden. Although it did not have the size of the pansies that had been the focus of the most recent decades, it was in letting go of the giant bloom in favor of concentrating on versatility that the violetta came to be. In 1894, during the Viola Conference at the Botanical Gardens in Birmingham, violettas were officially recognized as a class separate from the viola.

Viola ×williamsii, the violetta or miniature viola, is smaller than other violas, has a longer stem, is without rays, and is very fragrant. D. B. Crane, father to Howard Hamp Crane, both of whom authored several books on pansies, continued work on the cultivation of the violetta into the twentieth century. Among the best varieties available during the Edwardian era were 'Cynthia', pale blush to lilac with an oval form, yellow eye, and very long footstalks; 'Lavinia', blush lavender with veining a shade darker and an excellent creeping habit; and 'Thishe', beautiful pale blue flowers with long footstalks. Unfortunately, none of these varieties is still with us today.

As for the garden pansy—the pansy we know today versus the wild pansy— momentum began around 1812. Three gardeners, all within a few miles of one another, began to hybridize the wild *V. tricolor* that was growing in abundance in the gardens where they were employed. Mr. Thompson of Iver was one of those gardeners.

Pansy 'Thompson's King' from *A History and Description of the Different Varieties of the Pansey, or Heartsease, now in Cultivation in the British Gardens,* Sinclair & Freeman, 1835.

J. Freeman del.

Thompson's King.

W. Annan lith. 12 Gracechurch St

He worked for Lord (later to become Baron) Gambier, a retired Royal Navy rear admiral, who asked him to cultivate some common white-and-yellow heartseases in 1813. He was soon fully vested in his trials, having acquired all varieties he could find, which included a blue pansy from a Mr. Brown of Slough, Buckinghamshire, and a darker variety from Russia he bought from a gentleman whose name he could no longer recall. He saw his first worthwhile results in 1818 and continued to devote himself to raising the best varieties possible. In 1830, Thompson finally began to share them within the floristry community. He was quoted in great detail about his efforts in "History of the Heartsease," which appeared in the 1841 edition of *Floricultural Cabinet*, an original copy of which I am lucky enough to have in my own library. The first variety he felt confident taking cuttings from was named 'Lady Gambier', followed by 'Ajax', and later 'Thompson's King'. It was also Thompson, though by pure chance, who introduced the blotch so common among pansies today, having seen its little catlike face looking up at him from a self-sown heartsease growing wild in a neglected heath. He named the first blotched variety 'Thompson's Madora', followed by 'Victoria', then a dark bronze variety he named 'Flamium', along with 'Tartan', 'Vivid', and 'King of Beauties'. This would make 'Madora' the original blotched pansy, from which all varieties we know today are descended. More than thirty years of devoted cultivation resulted in Thompson being known as "the father of the heartsease" throughout southern England.

Just before Mr. Thompson received the *V. tricolor* from Lord Gambier, Lady Mary Elizabeth Bennet (who later became Lady Monck) passed some violas along to her father's gardener, a Mr. Richardson. She was the daughter of the 4th Earl of Tankerville, and her family grew violas in their garden at Walton-on-Thames. Mr. Richardson worked with Mr. Reed, a foreman from the nearby highly reputable nursery at Hammersmith, to produce twenty new and spectacular varieties that played an essential role in future cultivation of the pansy. Mr. Reed had also been given a large blue pansy from the Netherlands, thought to be the very same variety that Mr. Thompson was able to acquire from Mr. Slough. It is believed that it was James Lee, who had inherited the nursery at Hammersmith, that brought about the partnership between his foreman and Lady Bennet's gardener, as they lived just a few miles apart.

By 1835, no plant in history had experienced as rapid an increase in demand and cultivation as the pansy. That same year, London florists J. Sinclair and J. Freeman published *A History and Description of the Different Varieties of the Pansey, or Heartsease, now in Cultivation in the British Gardens.* Freeman illustrated twenty-

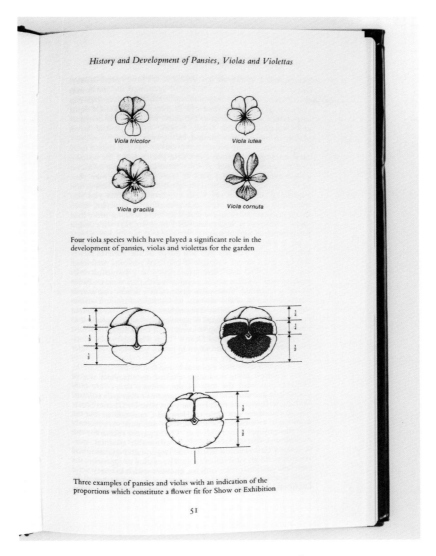

Illustration from *Pansies, Violas & Violettas: The Complete Guide*, R. Fuller, 1990.

four of the choicest varieties available at the time, in color and drawn from nature. Sinclair noted that several ladies of the nobility and of fashion had introduced some of the most noteworthy varieties, and raising new sorts had become a favorite study for them. He further stated, "It is curious to observe, that many who have spent nearly all their lives in the pleasures of a garden, have only until lately condescended to treat the poor Pansey in any other way than as a noxious weed."

The introduction of so many new varieties caused an absolute frenzy among early Victorian flower enthusiasts. Soon after, inferior lines of the most sought-after varieties were being sold, as many tried to cash in on the uninterrupted craze that lasted through 1838. Complaints of greedy florists flowering plants to death rather than preserving the varieties through propagation, along with the inability of everyone else to source and grow such varieties themselves, prompted jealousy and anger. (At this time, a florist was someone who cultivated, grew, and exhibited exceptional flowers, which is very different from how the term is used today.) It was in 1841, with the formation of the Hammersmith Heartsease Society, that strict rules and regulations governing the requirements for both exhibition and sales were finally enacted. Three years later, Scotland followed suit with the establishment of the Scottish Pansy Society, later to become known as the Scottish Viola and Pansy Association.

Show pansies continued to be grown among all classes, as those of limited income stood just as good a chance as the wealthy in competitive exhibitions. The pansy truly was, and still is, a flower for everyone. But what about those not interested in showing them? As all attention was paid to the flower itself, little thought was generally given to its growing habit. This resulted in exceptional varieties setting new standards for perfection in show but few varieties that were well suited for gardens. As many florists grew their specimens in small spaces, some having little to no garden at all, they were, for the most part, not adversely affected. But the new and highly rigid requirements made it significantly more difficult to expand cultivation of the pansy in England with the hope of making it more versatile for home gardeners and general enthusiasts.

Meanwhile, the English pansy, which made its way to France and Belgium in the early 1830s, had been undergoing cultivation there for years without the pedantic approach the English had taken. The French and Belgians felt no need to restrict the pansies as the English did, and during these years, they allowed natural cross-pollination to create flowers in varied colors, markings, shapes, and sizes. Jacques (James) Odier is responsible for the introduction of the Odier pansies and made significant strides in the development of the blotches on the lower petals. Mr. Odier was actually a banker by profession, not a nurseryman, but he had a passion for floriculture, and in addition to his pansies, he introduced some exceptional roses, among them the well-known Bourbon rose 'Louise Odier'.

John Salter, an English nurseryman who was particularly fond of pansies and had been growing them for years in Shepherd's Bush, set up a business in Versailles, France, in 1843. He took his best varieties with him and continued to grow them there for several years. After a number of trips to Belgium, Salter was now growing the most

Illustration of pansy 'Cleopatra' drawn from nature for *Amateur Gardening*, 1906.

VIOLA, OR TUFTED PANSY.

(Cleopatra.)

[Nat. Ord. Violaceæ, Violet Family.]

exceptional varieties from both countries, and it is these seeds that he carried with him on his return to England in 1848. The seeds were sown in his nursery, and the plants garnered considerable attention. This new Belgian pansy had won the favor of the public but was still unappealing to those whose eyes were trained on the English show pansies. Salter's imports prompted such scornful snarls from Victorian florists as "French rubbish" and "the gaudy sisters from Belgium" when he exhibited them at the Horticultural Society. Nonetheless, in 1851, he began to offer these varieties in his catalogs, beginning with these three: 'Caerulea Striata', of white and blue; 'Mars', in bronze and yellow; and 'Novelty', yellow striped with maroon. The next year, sixteen additional varieties were introduced, and in 1853, he offered a dozen more.

Belgian pansies had their first mention in the popular British horticultural periodical *Gardeners' Chronicle* in its November 3, 1849, issue. By 1852, John Downie of Downie, Laird, and Lang in Edinburgh exhibited six different varieties of the pansies in the Regent's Park gardens of the Royal Botanic Society, giving further credit to their merit. Downie went on to become one of the greatest cultivators and growers of these pansies in all of history. William Dean of Shipley, near Bradford in West Yorkshire, had also been cultivating Belgian pansies, particularly *V. lutea,* and he is credited with giving them a new name, the fancy pansy, a christening that he was quick to acknowledge: "I believe I may claim the credit of first using as a distinctive name for this new class of Pansies, the term "Fancy Pansy" in contradistinction to the Show Class; and although that veteran amongst our florists, Mr. John Downie, introduced years before—sorts which, for some years afterwards, were almost discarded, I think that I may be awarded the place of honour as father of the modern Fancy Pansy."

Eventually, enthusiasts in southern England started to lose interest in the show pansy, though it remained quite popular in the north and in Scotland. But within less than a decade of John Downie's planting in the Royal Botanic Gardens, Regent's Park, allegiances began to shift, and public admiration for the fancy pansy was growing. It was Scotland that brought the fancy pansy into full appreciation in the 1860s, which quickly became known as the home of the cultivated pansy.

While advances in the cultivation of the fancy pansy in the British Isles had shifted from England to Scotland, the flower continued to be cultivated without pause in France, where improvements were regularly being made. Among the most important growers was Auguste Joseph Miellez of Lille, located in the north of France near the Belgian border. He introduced some exceptional varieties, including 'Belle Esquermoise', 'Louise Miellez', and 'Distinction', before his death in March 1860. French publishers were active as well, with two important volumes on the pansy

Unknown variety of fancy pansy drawn from nature for *Les pensées: Histoire, culture, multiplication, emploi,* Barillet & Lesemann, 1869.

Three additional examples of the fancy pansy drawn from nature for *Les pensées: Histoire, culture, multiplication, emploi,* Barillet & Lesemann, 1869.

released in 1844, *La pensée* by Ragonot-Godefroy and *Traité sur la culture de la pensée* by Charles Louis Ponsort. Some twenty-five years later, in 1869, *Les pensées: Histoire, culture, multiplication, emploi* was published in Paris for the Société Botanique de France. It contained twenty-five extraordinary chromolithographs of pansies developed by Lesemann, head gardener at Hietzing near Vienna, that were considered the best varieties available at that time. Jean-Pierre Barillet, who was the director of gardens for the city of Paris, wrote the text for the book, which covered all aspects of the pansy. This volume offers an incredibly rare insight into the astonishing varieties cultivated in those years, and as only two hundred copies were printed, partisans of this exceptional flower are fortunate that a few of those copies still exist today for reference.

As with the English show pansy, the fancy pansy soon had its own set of restrictions when it came to exhibition. The form was required to be perfectly circular, the edges of the petals could have neither waves nor unevenness, and each variety must display a large blotch. This very closely mirrored the requirements for the English show pansy, which reached its peak of popularity in 1880. In fact, the only significant difference between the properties of a show and a fancy pansy was that the latter was allowed a broad spectrum of color. With regulations now in force for the fancy pansy, people started to take more interest in bedding pansies and violas (or tufted pansies). Bedding pansies of the day were direct descendants of the fancy pansies but smaller, more heavily branched, and more floriferous, making them ideal for growing in beds and borders.

The well-known British garden designer, horticulturist, and author Gertrude Jekyll loved pansies but did not care for show varieties. She once remarked how the show pansy judge has no eye, no brain, and no heart but instead a pair of compasses with which to describe a circle. Growers and authors for the Country Life library had also wearied of the stuffiness surrounding these flowers and expressed no sympathy for the show pansy in its little box at exhibitions. They did, however, still give credit to the growers in Scotland, noting that they had done exceptional work in the field of horticulture. Women were just as avid growers as men, and it is said that raised beds came about as an answer to dresses soiled from kneeling. (I have not been able to confirm this, but I certainly love the thought of it.)

In 1849, a writer in the *Gardeners' Chronicle* observed, "I know no plant so easy to cultivate as the pansy and at the same time so difficult to keep from year to year." By the late 1800s, it was officially the most popular flower grown from seed. The well-known Swiss Giants series was developed specifically with the intention of it coming true to seed, and the Roggli family spent half a century perfecting it at their home in Switzerland. It is because the pansy is so difficult to cultivate that we have seen so many varieties come and go. Developing varieties that would come true to seed would have been monumental at this time.

The Hammersmith Heartsease Society, which held its first show in 1841, was succeeded by the London Pansy and Viola Society in the late nineteenth century. In 1911, it became the National Viola and Pansy Society. This latter society had twenty-two council positions, thirty-six professional growers, and over four hundred members. It was soon followed by the formation of the North of England Pansy and Viola Society in 1915. These societies were devoted to furthering the growing, showing, and propagation of the best show and fancy pansies and of violas that met exhibition standards.

But in these early decades of the twentieth century, when men and women were suddenly forced to turn their attention to defending their country and ensuring their family's survival, the gentle care and hours needed to grow, tend, and meticulously cultivate the pansy could no longer be afforded. Many of the varieties cultivated in the nineteenth century disappeared during World War I, and the popularity of the pansy and the viola continued to wane after the war ended. D. B. Crane and Howard Hamp Crane published fresh editions of their books in 1922, hoping to reignite interest in the pansy and viola. They also staged an impressive display of violettas at the Chelsea Flower Show in 1939. Unfortunately, World War II closely followed. Howard Crane persisted, and in yet another attempt to garner enthusiasm and preserve their future, he published *Pansies and Violas for Exhibition and Garden* in 1951. Seven years later, prolific gardening writer Roy Genders published *Pansies, Violas and Violets,* his attempt to protect these treasured blooms. Trials and shows continued to be held throughout the 1960s and 1970s among those who loved these flowers most, but the changing trends in fashion, the shifting views of society, and two world wars had taken their toll.

So now, more than a century later, new varieties in nontraditional shades and patterns are finally starting to come back into favor. Demand is increasing and seed sales for pansies are on the rise. It is my hope that more people will see the pansy for all it truly is and has been. Incredible. Nostalgic. Purposeful. Historic. Essential. Here is a list of some popular varieties from centuries past, which serves as inspiration for varieties in the future.

'Black Knight' Large pansy of inky blackness
'Bronze Kintore' Dark bronze
'Brown and Bronze' Dark mahogany shades with a brown center
'Columbia' Ruffled petals of red, white, and blue (a favorite in 1903)
'Emperor William' Elegant deep blue (regarded as especially useful for bouquets)
'Giant Havana Brown' Old gold, fawn, and russet
'Giant Masterpiece' Large flowers with frilly and ruffled petals
'Giant Striped' Ruddy lilac with chamois and bronze
'Glencoe' Lower petals of rich mahogany, upper petals in copper
'Gloriosa Perfecta' Reddish steel blue with distinct red and white rim
'Irish Molly' Bronzy yellow bloom with a copper center (still available today)
'Jackanapes' Purple upper petals and yellow lower (named after
Gertrude Jekyll's monkey)
'Jennie Houston' Maroon shaded with gray
'Lawmuir' Rich crimson streaked with magenta
'Maggie Mott' Silvery mauve (considered a viola of exceptional beauty)
'Papilio' Violet blue with white edging (considered the best variety by H. H. Thomas)
'Peacock' Glorious and luminous bronze blue seen only in peacock feathers
'Silver Edged' Dark, rich, velvety purple with a distinct white edge
(especially good for cutting)
'Striped' Lilac, bronze, yellow on purple
'Thunder Cloud' Large, coal-black flowers with red-and-white rim
'Veined' Curious and beautiful
'Velvet Brown' Rich, velvety brown shades
'Wm. Penn' Light drab to brown and pearly gray

Illustration of a blue pansy, artist unknown, late nineteenth century

CHAPTER 2

Growing Pansies and Violas

Pansies and violas are some of the most approachable and easygoing flowers you can grow. They are also incredibly inclusive. Because of their hardy nature, they can be grown in almost all growing zones for at least a small part of the year. Additionally, they are admirably adaptable. There are so many places these sweet little flowers are willing to take up residence and keep you company, from woodlands, meadows, and hedges to gardens, small pots, and glasshouses. While they are one of the most common flowers cultivated, they are rarely grown to their full potential and have not been for many years.

British-born gardening writer H. H. (Harry Higgott) Thomas, author of *The Ideal Garden* (1911) and several other historic gardening books, observed that pansies will bloom from early May all the way through to November. He also noted that pansies are always better in their second year. I found this particularly interesting because I had always been taught that pansies are short-lived annuals, only good in spring and fall pots or landscaping. *Sweet Violets and Pansies,* edited by E. T. Cook and published by Country Life in 1903, challenged yet another convention I had been taught. While it confirmed that many sources suggest cool and shady spots as the most comfortable for pansies, it countered that advice by declaring that they flower best when exposed to full sun. This opinion was seconded by William Toole, a pansy specialist who bred pansies and sold seed through his Wisconsin company in the late nineteenth and early twentieth century. In his catalog he wrote, "My own experience does not permit me to favor shade. Shade during the afternoon heat can be ideal but too much and color and abundance suffer."

After trialing pansies extensively for several years, I, too, believe that pansies can and should be grown in full sun. Sun yields the healthiest plants and the most spectacular flowers. I have further learned that for pansies to thrive and bloom throughout summer, it is not a matter of sun versus shade but rather of soil, water, and health.

Pansy 'Delta Premium Persian Medley'

I live in growing zone 8a, one of two subsets of zone 8, which stretches from coastal Oregon and Washington State through central Texas and into the Carolinas. England, Ireland, Scotland, France, and Spain also have regions in this growing zone. The summers can be dry, and the last few summers have seen temperatures hovering in the upper eighties and nineties (lower to mid-thirties Celsius). My pansies continue to survive the summer heat as long as I care for them properly. That being said, as with many flowers, when temperatures rest above ninety degrees for long periods, my pansies suffer. Providing them with plentiful afternoon shade when temperatures peak will keep their roots happy. If you live in a warmer climate, cultivating pansies in the cooler months will help extend their flowering.

Deadheading and proactive bud removal play a huge role in the health of pansies, as the plants can essentially flower themselves to death. If planted out too late in spring, they will begin flowering before their roots are fully established and not stop until they are entirely depleted and unable to recover. Whether planting them in the spring or the autumn, it is important that they be given the opportunity to develop a strong root system. Deadheading encourages the plants to send energy to their root base rather than to spent flowers for seed production. Plus, providing the plants a full pause by removing all the blooms and buds once a month will help them to maintain vigor and continue to bloom healthily well into fall. I do this with my pansies each month throughout summer. I have found that deadheading is almost as essential for health and longevity as keeping them well watered.

A good way to test if your pansies will establish as perennials is to minimize the blooms and cut back the stems for the entire first year the plant is grown. It should accordingly develop an incredibly strong root base, allowing it not only to overwinter more successfully but also to put forth the most beautiful flush of flowers in its second year. Even if you prefer not to go an entire year without blooms, it is a good idea to cut pansies back when they show signs of fatigue and stress. If you are not growing for cutting, flowers that bloom in early spring can benefit from being cut back in June. This will allow them to rejuvenate and put forth another lovely flush of flowers in the fall. When my plants begin to show stress or when bloom size decreases, I cut them back to 1 to 2 inches (2.5 to 5 cm), right after the first joint. Apply a top dressing of well-rotted manure or compost, and you should see new basal shoots coming from the root base within a couple of weeks.

In addition to being told pansies need shade and are only good in spring or fall, I was taught that they require darkness to germinate. From the day I first started growing flowers, I have regularly tested what I've been taught. Most of the time, the way I was told to do it is indeed the most beneficial. But on occasion, I will find there is a better way for my circumstances and growing conditions, not necessarily making the information incorrect, just not ideal for me. And ever so rarely, I find the information is incorrect, though that often comes by happenstance rather than intention.

My first questions surrounding pansies needing darkness to germinate came about when I realized it was never mentioned in books written on pansies between the mid-nineteenth century and the late twentieth century. I had seen references to covering them lightly with soil so they didn't shift during watering but for no other reason. Still, I continued to keep them in darkness until I saw the first signs of germination, as that practice had proven very successful for me.

But one day, as I was looking over freshly sown seed trays hoping for the first peeks of green out of the moist brown soil, I noticed that I had missed lightly covering an entire tray. While my first inclination was to quickly cover the seeds with soil, I took

The cutting garden in late spring

a closer look and saw that the seeds were already germinating. This put them three to five days ahead in germination over the covered seeds. So I filled more trays and started several dozen more varieties to test the rates of germination when sown on the surface in full light. The results were again that the seeds left uncovered, in full light, germinated several days sooner than the seeds that were covered. I have since begun sowing all my pansies this way, and I have not had a single variety fail to germinate. While I have not found that it hinders their success to be lightly covered with soil, for me, it has proven unnecessary.

When growing pansies and violas, as with all types of flowers, there are year-round tasks that need to be addressed. This simple calendar serves as a starting point for growing, and it can be easily modified to fit your growing zone and goals as needed.

WINTER

- Start seeds, when applicable for your growing zone.
- Prepare your garden bed for the coming season. Weed and treat with lime if necessary. Sprinkle wood ash and bonemeal in a light dusting, then turn into the soil with well-rotted manure or compost and leaf mold.

EARLY SPRING

- Harden off your seedlings once they have four true leaves and transplant them into the garden. I do this in early March, as they can withstand the last few frosts.
- Begin to treat for slugs and snails.
- Uncover any overwintered violas and pansies that had a protective covering of leaves, mulch, or frost cloth and apply 2 inches (5 cm) of well-rotted manure or compost as a top dressing.
- Ensure all new transplants stay well watered, and remove early buds so they establish a healthy root base.
- Begin deadheading plants that were early to flower from fall sowing.

LATE SPRING

- Remove overgrowth from mature plants as necessary.
- Apply compost tea or seaweed fertilizer.
- Continue to be vigilant about protecting new growth from slugs and snails.
- Begin deadheading regularly once younger plants start flowering.
- Plant out any cuttings.

SUMMER

- Begin regularly aerating and loosening the soil in your beds.
- Cut back any fall-sown plants to the first joint if they are starting to show stress and apply 1 inch (2.5 cm) of well-rotted manure or compost as a top dressing.
- If you are growing plants for seed collection, now is the time to begin.

EARLY FALL

- Trim back any remaining old growth.
- Take cuttings from new basal shoots on desired varieties.

LATE FALL

- Begin preparations to protect your plants from piercing winds and extreme temperatures by covering them with straw, mulch, or frost cloth.

The cutting garden in early autumn

Ideal Soil Preparation and Maintenance

Pansies and violas are not too particular about the soil they grow in. Although they cannot survive in dry sand or in wet clay, they can often be found sprouting up between the cracks in a sidewalk or among the rocks filling a gravel driveway. Even so, surviving and thriving are not synonymous. If you want your pansies and violas to put forth the finest flowers possible, you will want to provide them with the best environment possible. If you are unsure about what kind of soil you have, test kits are widely available and relatively inexpensive. The ideal growing medium for pansies and violas is rich, loamy soil, which is fairly easy to create.

I had never heard the term *loam* until I began growing flowers on a large scale. If you are also unfamiliar with it, it is essentially well-balanced soil that contains equal parts sand, clay, and humus. Humus, which is also known as organic fertilizer, consists of vegetation or animal matter that releases nutrients into the soil, improving both the texture and moisture retention. It is the most important component when growing pansies. It is absolutely imperative for sufficient moisture control, and you really cannot have too much of it. Humus differs from compost in that it is essentially the end result, having already decomposed, while compost is still in the process of decomposing.

Pansies require consistently cool and moist soil deep at their roots, especially in summer. If the soil cannot sufficiently hold water, their roots will turn upward and dry out quickly. Well-rotted cow or horse manure is an excellent component in creating loam, as it allows the soil to hold adequate moisture in the summer yet drain freely in winter. You can tell the manure is rotted and ready when all the straw is broken down and the smell has subsided. If it is still steaming or smelly, it is still breaking down, and you must not use it. When sourcing manure, keep in mind the diet of the animals producing it. If the animals have consumed grass or hay that has been treated with herbicides, those chemical products can pass through to the manure and have an adverse effect on your plants. I recommend speaking directly with the farmer supplying your manure to make sure no herbicides or other chemicals have been used in the feed. Don't be tempted to use chicken manure. While it is good in compost piles, it should not be added directly to the soil.

It's through good-quality soil and deep watering that pansies will continue to bloom from spring until fall. Because the most spectacular flowers are achieved through a full day's sun, it's imperative to keep the roots healthy all summer long. But because the root systems of pansies stay rather compact, they will quickly deplete the soil.

Regular feeding will compensate for this. Manure, bonemeal, and seaweed fertilizer are all excellent sources of nutrients. During the growing season, I do my best to spray my flowers and soil weekly with a compost tea or liquid seaweed fertilizer. I also use an organic sprinkle fertilizer before planting and then again mid-season.

Plants require food rich in nitrogen, phosphate, and potassium (NPK). If you know how to listen to your plants, they will tell you what they need. A nitrogen deficiency can display as pale leaves and weak stems. Adding well-rotted manure is a great way to add nitrogen back into the soil. If you add too much, however, your plants will produce significantly more foliage than flowers. A purplish tint on the leaves of your pansies may mean insufficient phosphates. Phosphates are what promote good root development, and bonemeal is an excellent source. Mixing in bonemeal before transplanting and adding it throughout the season as needed will ensure your pansies have healthy roots. If the leaves are turning yellow or brown and the flowers seem inferior in color, they may need a boost of potash potassium. Wood ash is a great

Pansies growing in ideal soil

source and one I mix into my pansy beds every winter. As we use a wood-burning fireplace to heat our home in the cooler months, I have a steady supply of ash ready by January. Be sure to use ash from clean-burning, untreated wood only and keep it stored in a very dry place, as it is soluble. Although it is best to mix the wood ash into the soil in winter so it has time to rest, it can be added directly when pH levels drop. When adding to boost pH, no more than 1 to 1½ ounces (30 to 45 g) per square yard (m) is recommended.

Midwinter is the ideal time to amend your soil, assuming the ground is not entirely frozen. When growing pansies, 9 inches (23 cm) of rich loamy soil is ideal. Leaf mold is a great base layer and is easy to make. It is essentially decayed leaves that over time turn into a rich, crumbly, dark brown or black matter with a strong, earthy smell. You can expedite the process by adding grass clippings. Spread a layer of well-rotted manure on top of the leaf mold. Each of the first two layers should be about 1½ inches (4 cm) thick. The top 6 inches (15 cm) should be a good mix of garden soil and compost. Dust with bonemeal and wood ash and turn over thoroughly. Because pansies severely deplete the soil, it is recommended to rotate in a vegetable crop or replace the entire 9 inches (23 cm) of soil every three years.

Turning and aerating the soil regularly throughout the season does two things: it turns up insects and pests that may be hiding below ground so they can be controlled naturally by birds, and it keeps the soil from forming a crust that may inhibit good water absorption. Alternatively, mulch is a great way to help keep the soil cool and moist throughout the growing season. Spreading a layer of mulch about 1 inch (2.5 cm) thick around pansies will prove beneficial, though you must be careful to keep it from coming into contact with the stems. As mulch helps retain moisture in the soil, trapping moisture at the stem base can promote disease and rot. Accordingly, I do not mulch my full beds of pansies, which are grown close together for cut flowers. Pansies should be watered regularly in the evenings, applying the water slowly and to a depth of 4 to 5 inches (10 to 13 cm). Deep watering encourages deep roots.

Pansy 'Chianti Mix'

Starting from Seed

Pansies can be found just about anywhere plants are sold. You can buy starts in person or have plugs and seeds shipped through the post. I prefer to start all my pansies from seed, as I grow them primarily for cut flowers. It's been said that starting pansies from seed can be difficult, but I have found that by following a few key steps, it can be easily mastered.

There are two factors to be aware of when you begin growing pansies from seed. First, some pansy seeds can be expensive compared with other types of flower seeds. There are several reasons for this, but it's primarily because of how labor-intensive it is to obtain high-quality seed true to variety. The second factor is that certain specialty pansy seeds are notorious for their low germination rates. Not all varieties are this way, but some of the hybrids are. I have grown accustomed to this, and the varieties I know will germinate at lower rates, I offset by sowing additional seed.

Most sources recommend that pansy and viola seeds be used within a year of purchase. I store all my seeds in a sturdy, airtight plastic food-storage container in my flower cooler, which maintains its temperature between 36° and 40°F (2° and 4°C). As a result, some of my pansy and viola seeds have germinated well at five years old, despite the fact that most seeds are regarded as viable for only two to three years. It is not just storage that affects seed viability. Genetics and quality play a role as well. Not all seeds from all varieties will keep for years, of course. But I have found it's always worth doing a couple of sowings to determine viability before discounting older seed.

If you are new to growing flowers from seed, here are a couple of tips that have made the seed-sowing process much more enjoyable and convenient on my own little farm. Perhaps they will help you find not only what works best for you but also help alleviate some frustration or discomfort along the way.

First, make your space. By this I mean designate an area where you are able to work freely and without judgment for the mess that is assured to ensue. It doesn't need to be a huge space, especially in the beginning. When I first started growing flowers from seed, I filled a handful of cell trays in my driveway and then sowed the seeds at my kitchen table. After a couple of years, I sold my Aprilia RSV 1000 R motorcycle (I called her Francesca) to buy my first greenhouse. Where I had once taken to long, winding roads and leaning into corners to allow my body and soul to release stress and decompress, I now found a calmer, quieter form of release in growing flowers. The greenhouse I purchased is very modest. It is only eight by twelve feet (2.4 by 3.6 m) and not particularly well structured. In fact, I had to devise a special tie-down system to keep it from blowing away in the wind storms we often get here on Camano Island. I will upgrade it one day, but for now it meets my needs.

Second, take your time finding your preferred tools and do it with joy. In the beginning, I used a large, black plastic tub and the garden hose for filling seed trays. It wasn't pleasant, and it usually left my back aching and my hands freezing, but the combo worked well. The tub was repurposed or stored in the garage between seasons until the plastic eventually cracked, forcing me to find a replacement. My farm, even now, is so small that a large, permanent potting table has not proven necessary. But rather than buy another plastic tub that would likely crack and need to be discarded within a few seasons, I purchased an old French enamel baby bath that I found at a local vintage fair. It is not only indestructible but also the perfect height and meant to hold water, so I never have to worry about it leaking. Plus, instead of using cold water from the garden hose, I fill it with buckets of warm water from the sink, a change that makes preparing trays so much more enjoyable. Finally, it stores conveniently away in the eaves of my garden shed when not in use.

I prefer longevity over convenience, and I prefer comfort over misery. By making little changes over the past few years that suit my own preferences, the entire process of sowing seeds has become enjoyable from beginning to end. Buckets, watering cans, and many garden tools are still made essentially the same way they were many years ago. Buying secondhand or vintage is not only environmentally friendly but also allows you to curate a special collection of well-made tools that suit your taste and will often save you quite a bit of money. My favorite watering can is an old brass Haws with a very fine rose that couldn't be more perfect for starting seeds. Haws still makes the very same watering can today. Mine is made so well that it will probably last longer than I will. I take comfort in knowing I will never have to replace it.

Pansies and violas can be sown any time of the year as long as you can provide the proper environment for germination. When sown in January, they will flower in mid-spring, and as summer progresses, the stems will be drawn out, making them ideal for cutting. Sowing in early spring allows for flowering from midsummer all the way through fall. In the southern states, a late-July sowing with planting out in September may yield flowers from October through most of winter.

My little garden shed and my sweet dog, Coco

If you intend to sow pansies in fall for overwintering, you will need to ensure they have a well-established root base before the freezing temperatures set in. To give them the best chance, I recommend sowing seeds in May, transplanting out in July, and removing all the buds and blooms until September. Alternatively, Helena Ely Rutherford, author of several fantastic books, including *A Woman's Hardy Garden* (1903), preferred to transplant hers out the first week in September. With daily watering and a little protective covering beginning in November if necessary for your climate, they should be ready to flower by March. For the most part, when planted in fall, pansies should come into bloom by April.

If sowing seeds when the temperatures are warm, you will need to keep their environment cool. Germination rates suffer dramatically when temperatures are maintained above 75°F (24°C). I sow my pansies in succession, and when sowing during warmer months, I keep them indoors where the temperatures are cooler until they are ready for transplanting out. In the winter, in contrast, I move them into my unheated greenhouse as soon as germination occurs, where they continue to grow hardily in temperatures much cooler than in my home. The best way to find what works well for you and your climate is to try a few scenarios and modify accordingly.

SUPPLIES NEEDED FOR STARTING PANSIES AND VIOLAS FROM SEED

- Plug/seed-starting trays (I use 72-cell trays with flat 1020 trays without holes)
- Humidity domes to cover seed trays
- Plant labels and permanent, weatherproof marker
- High-quality seed-starting mix
- Potting table, tub, or container for mixing soil
- Fine-spray watering can
- Artificial lighting for indoor growing or a greenhouse
- Vermiculite (optional)

Top: Have your watering and labeling implements on hand before you start sowing.
Bottom: Label your trays as you sow.

How to Start

1. Using a table, tub, or similarly adequate container, mix your seed-starting soil with enough water to make it thoroughly wet but not overly saturated. When gently pinched between your fingers, it should stick together but not drip with water.

2. Fill your cell trays with the starting mix. I use my bare hands, pushing the soil gently into the cells and smoothing it out. Eliminate any air pockets by firmly tapping your full seed trays on the ground or a countertop a few times.

3. Sow one to two seeds on the surface of each cell. You can leave them uncovered, as germination occurs most quickly and effectively when left uncovered, or you can cover them with a very light layer of vermiculite or soil.

4. Give the seeds a gentle, very fine watering, then cover them with humidity domes. Alternatively, bottom water the seeds by filling the under tray with a small amount of water and letting the soil absorb it from the bottom up. If you decide on bottom watering, it is important that the surface stays moist. However, make sure there is not so much water that it cannot be fully absorbed between waterings.

5. Place the trays in adequate lighting, whether indoors with artificial lighting or in a greenhouse. The ideal temperature for germination is 60° to 68°F (15° to 20°C). Anything warmer than 70°F (21°C) will cause germination rates to suffer.

6. Keep the soil moist. The most important factor in good germination is that the soil not dry out. Pansies and violas generally take 7 to 14 days to germinate. That being said, I have had some varieties take well over 30 days. It's worth being patient.

7. Once the seeds have germinated, the humidity domes should be removed to aid in airflow and decrease the risk of disease or fungal growth. Regularly check the seedlings to ensure they never dry out. If you are growing the seedlings indoors until they are ready for planting out, ensure they continue to receive adequate air circulation.

8. When the seedlings are about 1 inch (2.5 cm) tall and have developed at least four true leaves, it is safe to harden them off and transplant them out. Hardening them off is achieved by gradually acclimating them to their permanent location for a few hours each day over the course of a week. Midmorning is usually the best window of time, as direct intense sun and abrasive winds can be damaging in the first few days.

If your seedlings look long and leggy like the photo above, they are not receiving enough light.

Top left: Pansy seeds are very tiny.
Top right: The first signs of germination
Bottom two: Pansy seedlings showing seed leaves and their first true leaves

Transplanting into the Garden or Containers

Pansies and violas can withstand light frost even when they are young, so they can be transplanted out a few weeks before most other seedlings in the spring. They are typically ready when they are about 1 inch (2.5 cm) tall and have developed at least four true leaves. You may need to take care in protecting them from harsh winds, though, depending on your climate. A good wind is more likely to kill off tender, young plants than frigid temperatures and frost.

Soil should be allowed time to settle naturally before planting, which is why soil prep in winter is so important. (It is equally important to pat down the soil firmly before sowing seeds directly into the garden.) Over and above that, you can add some manure a week prior and sprinkle 2 ounces (55 g) of bonemeal per square yard (m) just before transplanting to assist the seedlings' first flush. To help prevent transplant shock, add some of the same seed-starting soil to the prepared bed or pot where the seedlings will be taking up new residence.

When transplanting pansies and violas, do not use a dibber, as their roots should never be constricted. If you are unfamiliar with a dibber, it is a pointed hand tool used for making holes when planting out bulbs and seedlings. Although it is a wonderful tool, you will want to use a hand shovel, or trowel, for pansies. Try to disturb the roots as little as possible when lifting the seedings from the seed trays. My preferred method is to use a landscape staple in a manner similar to chopsticks, which causes very little disturbance. Another popular tool among growers for this step is a butter knife.

Should you be a bit behind in planting out—which has happened to me on more than one occasion—be sure to remove any buds or flowers you find before transitioning the seedlings into the ground. As painful as this is to do, it is so important that all their energy go to their roots at this time. Spacing is a matter of preference, but I recommend planting them no more than 4 inches (10 cm) apart when growing for cut flowers and 9 to 12 inches (23 to 30 cm) apart when growing in landscaping.

Pansies can endure some shade, which is also beneficial in keeping the soil cool and moist, but they bloom most beautifully with at least six full hours of sun every day. The best way to achieve cool moisture at their root base is through regular slow, deep watering.

Transplant with care so as to not compact or damage the roots.

Pollinators love pansies because they provide pollen and nectar when not much else is in bloom.

While the greatest threat to tender seedlings is inadequate watering, slugs and snails are a close second. As soon as you transplant your seedlings out, you will need to treat for these insatiable garden residents or your entire crop could be lost in just one night.

When transplanting seedlings into pots or other containers, the same general rules apply. The soil needs to provide both ample water retention and adequate drainage. I have learned the best mix for pots is two parts good soil, one part leaf mold, one part manure, and just enough sharp sand to keep the mix porous. Alternatively, pansies can be sown directly into the pots you intend to keep them in. I do this with my terra-cotta pots, as it saves me from having to disturb their roots while transplanting. It is even more crucial to regularly water pansies and violas in pots than in beds, and the pots must never dry out. If you are using a terra-cotta pot, always water the pot along with the plant, as the pot itself absorbs a lot of moisture. Pot-raised pansies and violas can still be grown for long stems. Trellises are an option, as the plants will climb upward with some support. If you want your plants to be fuller rather than trailing, continue to cut them back as they lengthen, and they will instinctively send out new basal shoots.

Pansies among Vegetables

In addition to being well suited for both flower gardens and containers, pansies are great additions to a vegetable garden. As they are an edible flower, they can be harvested right alongside your crops. Pansies also aid in weed control, and it is much more beautiful to have them sprawling about between the lettuce and carrots than it is unpleasant, suffocating weeds. When planted among tomatoes, they will grow right up within the cages alongside them. This method yields stems long enough to fill jars for adorning the dinner table. Alternatively, they can be grown at the base of your snap peas, where they can trellis just as they do with sweet peas in the flower garden.

Incorporating pansies among your vegetables is an ideal option when you don't have the space or desire for a garden devoted to cutting flowers. You'll benefit from all the joy these blooms provide without the additional maintenance.

Pansies and Pollinators

As pansies and violas are some of the first flowers to bloom in the spring and some of the last to remain in bloom throughout the fall, they are excellent for supporting pollinators. My pansies and violas are always abuzz with bees and butterflies, but if you want to grow them specifically for pollinators, I recommend planting the varieties that have not been hybridized. A number of articles have expressed concern that hybridized pansies may contain longer nectar tubes, making it difficult for bees to reach the nectar, while violas and open-pollinated pansies have long been well suited for supporting our little winged friends.

I grow ample flowers specially to support pollinators, such as bee balm, lavender, and catmint, but many do not come into bloom until spring gets going. Pansies and violas are already there and waiting as soon as bees begin to emerge from their hives. Bees are always flying around my violas when I am out deadheading, and I am quite fond of the company they provide. They have never once bothered or stung me, and it is truly fascinating to watch them work.

Growing Pansies and Violas for Cut Flowers

For decades, pansies have been deemed unsuitable as cut flowers for arrangements and floral work, but it wasn't always that way. I was desperate to know the facts behind the pansy's disappearance from mainstream floristry, so I researched and read all I could until the mystery was solved—or at least mostly solved.

Using pansies as cut flowers is not a new trend or a recent discovery, having been grown avidly for this purpose from the late nineteenth through the mid-twentieth century. The first documented flower shop in the United States was established around 1851, and at that time and for the following decades, all cut flowers were from local growers, as there was no means to keep them fresh in transport. As the number of flower shops grew, pansies quickly became part of the regular inventory. In the 1935 edition of *The Standard Cyclopedia of Horticulture,* author L. H. Bailey verifies this trend, noting that pansies were being grown extensively for cut flowers throughout the country. Pansies are an accessible flower and have remarkable longevity in vases, so it is understandable that they did so well for so long with florists. But why did they disappear from florists' shops?

It wasn't until the 1950s that the floral industry began to shift away from locally grown flowers. With advances in transportation, specifically refrigerated trucks, flowers could be grown in more ideal climates. Northern growers ceased production, as the expense of operating greenhouses in colder climates was too great. At one point, California came to command almost the entire cut-flower industry of the United States. This pushed out the small-scale growers and resulted in only a handful of large companies meeting the demand. Losing small growers meant losing pansies as a cut flower. By the 1960s, international trade was a factor, and flowers were being grown and shipped all over the world. The increase in availability from imported flowers was devastating to the large-scale US growers. Many of them shifted all of their production from cut flowers to plants grown for bedding and landscaping. It was during this time that small-scale flower farmers were once again able to establish themselves.

By the 1990s, many customers had grown tired of red roses, pink carnations, and white lilies. They wanted different colors and different flowers from what was being offered commercially. Local growers were able to provide customers with a variety of unusual blooms in varying shades and exotic shapes. Too delicate to ship, these flowers could only be sourced from the surrounding farms. They didn't have to spend days packed in boxes, where they could wilt and discolor, and they did not need to be treated with chemicals, preservatives, or pesticides. Beautiful, natural, fresh, organically grown, and seasonal, locally produced cut flowers were once again available. But by this time, the pansy's usefulness as a cut flower was long forgotten.

I find this timeline particularly interesting when looking back at the books written on pansies and violas. Understandably, most were written before World War I, which saw the loss of a great many varieties as there was no longer ample labor to cultivate them. The next truly substantial book wasn't published until 1958, several years after additional varieties were lost during World War II, and shortly after consideration of pansies as cut flowers ceased with the demise of small-scale growers. Some three decades later, in 1990, Rodney Fuller's *Pansies, Violas & Violettas: The Complete Guide* was published by The Crowood Press in Wiltshire, England. This is, in my opinion, the most comprehensive book ever written on pansies and violas, and it makes a strong case for the need to work actively in preserving their future. Yet even in this extraordinary account, their use as a cut flower is only briefly mentioned.

As noted earlier, during the peak of the pansy's cultivation in the second half of the nineteenth century, popular opinion surrounding these sweet-faced flowers started to split. The florists of the time, who grew and exhibited the flowers, were interested in furthering the pansy for show purposes alone, while small-scale gardeners and passionate enthusiasts of the flower embraced the many new and varied traits and colors along with the long branching stems that they found performed exceptionally well in vases. To this day, pansy lovers are divided into two camps: those who love the perfectly proportioned, vibrantly colored, compact little plants with the characteristic blotch, and those who embrace the natural elongating and broad range of possibilities the flower possesses when grown freely in its more natural habit. I love the pansies and violas whose petals vary in shape, boast colors in unlikely shades, and grow with long stems reminiscent of their origin.

The pansy was once highly esteemed and considered elegant and appropriate for filling a vase for even the most prestigious of occasions, and it is still capable of playing this role today. In her 1899 book *Wood and Garden,* famed British horticulturist Gertrude Jekyll supported this use, writing, "Then there are Pansies, delightful things in a room, but they should be cut in whole branches of leafy stem and flower and bud." Several authors included in *Sweet Violets and Pansies,* published in 1903, concurred. In addition to discussing the fragrance as fresh and wholesome without the almost disagreeable sweetness of the violet, they proclaim that cutting the flowers of the pansy is a blessing, and those who do not use these flowers for cutting have lost sight

Viola 'Arkwright Ruby'

of one of their best virtues. They went on to add that pansies have little to no value when the flowers are picked off singly, as all the natural beauty of the flower is lost this way. But when the shoots with flower and foliage are cut of sufficient length, they are very beautiful indeed.

Along with its great beauty, the cut pansy brings exceptional vase life. When picked as a single flower on the pedicel (the stalk that joins the base of a solitary flower to the main stem), they last only a day or two. However, when picked in whole with the long primary stem, leaves, flowers and buds intact, they will last from two weeks to a month. With frequent fresh water and removal of spent blooms, not only will the formed buds open but new buds will form and continue to open as well. I left a jar of long-stemmed black pansies in my kitchen window and was astonished to find that not only did the buds that were present on the flowers when I cut them fully open, but the stems continued to grow with new buds forming and blooming. They lasted almost five weeks on my sunny sill before some dreaded spider mites found them and did them in.

It is the first full flush on pansies that produces the largest and most brilliant flowers. As the temperatures warm and summer carries on, the blooms will get slightly smaller and stems will lengthen. Bloom size is still plenty substantial through early summer, and mid-June through mid-July is when I harvest the largest crop of long-stem pansies in my own garden. These are flowers from January seeds as well as some from fall-sown seeds. Because you reduce the number of flowers the plant produces when growing and cutting with long stems, it is ideal to do succession planting if you are looking to harvest a substantial number of long stems from spring through fall.

As with all cut flowers, pansies and violas do best when harvested in the cool morning hours while they are thoroughly hydrated. Cut them close to the base, right at the first joint. This allows for as long a stem as possible and for the plant to recover after cutting by producing additional basal shoots. Remove all the leaves that will fall below the water line, and promptly place the flowers in cold water in a flower cooler or a cool room out of direct sunlight for a minimum of two to four hours before arranging. Pansies need to be thoroughly hydrated and recovered before being used in floral design, particularly wedding bouquets. If using for an out-of-water bouquet, ensure they have had ample time in cool water, and keep the bouquet in a vase when not in use for the ceremony and photography.

Here are the methods I have found most productive for growing and training pansies and violas for cut flowers.

Pansies grown for cut flowers in a raised bed

GROWING IN RAISED BEDS

This is how I first began growing and trialing stem length. I began with one 4-by-10-foot (1.2-by-3-m) bed and now have four beds devoted entirely to pansies. My beds are 12 inches (30 cm) high, and I fill them with loamy soil that is 8 to 9 inches (20 to 23 cm) deep once it has settled. I plant the pansies 2 to 4 inches (5 to 10 cm) apart. That way, they all grow together using one another for support as they lengthen upward. I usually see stem length of 10 to 16 inches (25 to 40 cm) with this method.

If you have limited space or if you prefer a smaller structure, bulb crates or similar-style containers are a good option. I have not used them myself, as I have always had access to raised beds, but I've known several flower farmers who have found great success with these methods.

COMBINING WITH OTHER FLOWERS

Pansies are known to self-seed, and it was through this that I first had pansies growing among my roses. They grew even taller with the canopy of rose branches than they did in raised beds. Pansies grown between roses provide welcome color while the roses are between flushes and help suppress weeds, and the two plants do not negatively interfere with each other.

Several self-seeding pansy and viola varieties also grew among my annual phlox and amaranth. I have found their maximum stem length when grown among other tall flowers is 16 to 24 inches (40 to 61 cm). I continue to plant pansies with my roses and phlox every year in addition to sowing them in their own dedicated raised beds.

Several years ago I transplanted a particular pansy into a pot so I could isolate it and collect seed. As it lengthened, I provided it with a little trellis to help support the stems. I noticed it grew quite well with this ongoing form of upward support. The next season, I began growing pansies along the entire base of my sweet peas, and many of the varieties began to climb along the trellis. 'Chianti Mix', 'Moulin Rouge', Imperial 'Antique Shades', and 'Can Can' maintained stems of 16 to 20 inches (40 to 50 cm) with this structured support. The black varieties, in particular, along with Nature 'Mulberry Shades', averaged stems of 22 to 24 inches (56 to 61 cm). 'Arkwright Ruby' climbed over 36 inches (91 cm). I remember reading in Howard Hamp Crane's book *Pansies & Violas for Exhibition and Garden* that a hybridizer in the 1940s found a variety that could climb upward of 48 inches (122 cm) on a trellis, but that it was deemed impractical at the time, and the variety was not further cultivated. The story leaves me curious as to the potential for climbing pansies.

Pansies grown for cut flowers at the base of sweet peas

Collecting Your Own Seed

Pansies and violas are both highly efficient at self-seeding and easy to collect seed from. In nature, bees, moths, and flies hunt the nectar located in the spur behind the lower petal and feed on pollen released from the anthers. In doing so, they add pollen from other blooms they've visited to the lip on the upper side of the stigma where the spur joins the petal, resulting in cross-pollination.

The best time to collect seed is in July, from the plants that produced the strongest and most spectacular blooms throughout May and June. Seedpods, which will droop slightly once the petals are shed, eventually straighten out and turn upright again as they ripen. When they are a ruddy brown, they are ready to harvest. Collect the pedicel stalk and pod together in a brown paper bag, as at this point, the pods are capable of bursting open and spraying seed.

Seeds collected from hybrid varieties will not come back true. The new plants can pull traits from either parent, so the blooms will not look like the flower from which the seed was collected. They also tend to be less vigorous, and the more unique hybrids may produce little to no seed at all. This doesn't mean it's not worth saving some of these seeds to see what you get. I have had some really wonderful faces appear in my garden as a result of self-seeding and collecting my own seed, and if you have the space, I highly encourage you to give it a try. It makes the entire growing season feel like an ongoing treasure hunt.

While it can be fun to let nature take its course and see the new varieties that result from self-seeding or from seeds collected in your own garden, intentionally breeding new varieties is an entirely different undertaking, and hand-pollinating is an extremely delicate task to master. Breeding new varieties requires full isolation. It's also important that all rogue or inferior plants be removed immediately and continuously and that seed is collected from only the healthiest plants. You will want to discern the new varieties' worth based on several criteria, including how floriferous it is, the shape of the petals and the flower as a whole, if the head hangs or stands upright, if there is consistency in the color or patterns, if it is fragrant, if the foliage is healthy and vibrant, if it is vigorous and disease tolerant, and how it performs in varying climates, in addition to many other factors. Most breeders spend well over a decade perfecting just a single new variety, and the future of the pansy depends on passionate growers and their continued efforts. If you think this is something you are interested in, I highly encourage you to look into it further.

The progression of the seed pod

Propagation by Cuttings, Root Division, and Layering

While the best method for growing pansies will always be seed, it is possible to propagate them through cuttings. Increasing stock in certain violas can also be very easily achieved through root division, as long as they have plenty of dense roots to divide. Layering is another option, but it is not used often.

The advantage to cuttings from pansies, as with cuttings from all flowers, is that you get an exact duplicate of the original. As hybrid pansies do not produce seed true to variety, cuttings are often the only option if you want to increase your stock on a new variety that has grown through self-seeding or natural pollination in your garden. When promising new faces first appeared among my pansies, I tried isolation and seed collection as well as cuttings to increase stock on these novel beauties. The seed I collected, as expected, did not produce the same variety again. If not for the cuttings, the varieties would have come and gone in one season.

It is not abnormal for a young pansy to put out only one shoot. Once you know you want to propagate it, it is essential that you remove all further flowers and buds to build up the root base and encourage new basal shoots. It is these new shoots that will be the source of your cuttings. While it may seem a horrid task to remove the flowers on a plant you are excited about, it gives it the best chance of survival.

In the book *The Flower Garden*, published in 1838, there is a small section titled "Lost Sorts." In it, author Charles MacIntosh discusses losing a dark bronze variety that was better than any others in cultivation at the time. I've come across many old seed catalogs and reference books remarking on the vast number of varieties and colors of pansies readily available at the time. I wish they were still being grown, but almost all of them are now lost sorts as well. It is vital that care be taken to establish a plant's health in its roots and the growth of fresh shoots for cuttings over allowing it to flower. As MacIntosh observed, "Many varieties possessing great merits one year, were nowhere to be found the following. The florist, being ever eager to have as many flowers on one plant as possible, suffers the plant to produce flowers until it becomes completely exhausted. It is like grasping at the shadow and losing the substance." I don't think it's possible to define the tragedy of a lost variety any better than this.

Cuttings taken from healthy basal shoots

TAKING CUTTINGS

Some pansy varieties are better suited for cuttings than others, but it's always worth a try. I am not well experienced in propagation through cuttings, but my self-taught efforts have yielded a good success rate, which supports the case that pansy cuttings are relatively easy to master. Cuttings should only be taken from strong, healthy shoots when the weather is damp and the plants are well hydrated. This is the timeline I follow for cuttings in my growing zone (8a).

- In early July, aggressively trim off the top flowering growth down to the first joint of any mature plants you want to take cuttings from, taking care not to damage any new basal shoots underneath. Once the stems flower, they become hollow and cannot be used for cuttings. For the best chances of success, you want to cut only solid new basal shoots.
- In September or early October, when the shoots are sufficiently mature, you should be able to obtain healthy cuttings. The cutting should be 2 to 3 inches (5 to 7.5 cm) long and taken just below a stem joint. Cut with a very sharp blade, and then trim off all bottom leaves or remove them by gently pulling up so as not to tear fragile stems. Insert half of the cutting into a good propagation mix that has been well moistened. The cutting should be no more than 1 to 1½ inches (2.5 to 4 cm) tall above the soil, with 1½ inches (4 cm) below the soil. You can also dip the cuttings into a rooting agent first, but it is not usually necessary with pansies. As long as the cuttings are healthy, they do well developing roots.
- Cover the cuttings with a humidity dome until the roots form. It will normally take about two weeks in temperatures of 60° to 65°F (15° to 18°C), but it's best to keep them in a humid, well-ventilated environment for three to four weeks. Be sure to pinch all new buds that may develop. September and early October cuttings should be overwintered in a greenhouse or equally protected space until planting in March or April.
- If you have taken your cuttings during the summer months of July or August, you can plant them either directly into a well-prepared bed or into other areas of the garden. They should still have sufficient time to establish before frost sets in. If planting the cuttings directly, it is vital that the soil be kept moist at all times and that the tender cuttings be fiercely protected from slugs and snails. You will also want to shade them from the afternoon scorch. Turning a terra-cotta pot over them during the latter half of the day in the first couple of weeks will help them get established.
- About a month after your plants are well established in the garden, apply some manure and leaf mold into and around their crown.

Top: When plants become scraggly, trim back to first joint.
Bottom: A layer of compost can now be applied, and new basal shoots should appear within one to two weeks.

ROOT DIVISION

Root division is an option only with certain varieties of violas. The plant must have a bushy base and an ample root system to be divided. For example, *Viola cornuta,* which spreads at its roots, is a good choice for this propagation method. Established plants can be divided in spring or fall, but spring is preferred because there is normally an abundance of new growth. If you prefer to divide in fall, wait until the flowers start to produce smaller blooms before dividing. When growing violas for root division, you will need to increase the spacing significantly beyond what you would use when growing them for cut flowers. A minimum of 12 inches (30 cm) apart is recommended. This way you will be able to dig them freely without risk to the surrounding plants.

- With larger plants, gently lift them with a pitchfork and carefully separate into several smaller clumps. Then replant each division right back into the prepared soil. Ensure each clump has ample roots.
- If the plant has dense roots and plenty of shorter new growth, smaller divisions will be possible and are an efficient way to increase plant stock quickly, as they, too, can be immediately replanted.
- If the plant is smaller and does not have an ample root system, small divisions can be made following the same care taken with cuttings, allowing them to establish a new root system before transplanting back into the garden.

LAYERING

Layering is the least common method of propagation, but it is relatively simple to do. For plants that lack sufficient growth for cuttings or an ample root base for division, you can try layering long branches for new growth. This involves laying the stem outward across the soil and burying a joint in the soil so it roots from there as a new plant. Layering is successful only if moisture is continuous, and it should be done only between mid-June and mid-September.

- Remove all the buds from the elongated stem you are using for propagation, then make a small, clean cut below the joint you will be covering. Be sure you do not cut through the stem entirely. If available, apply some rooting powder or gel before gently securing the joint and covering it with compost and dirt.
- Keep the area moist at all times and roots should form in three to four weeks. Once rooted, the branch can be severed from the mother plant.

Root division is possible with only certain varieties of violas.

Common Diseases and Pests

Pansies and violas are susceptible to some of the same diseases and pests as many other flowers. As with fighting illness in all living things, preventing such problems is always better than trying to treat them once they have established themselves.

Everything on our little farm is grown organically to avoid exposing our children, our pets, or our local wildlife to anything harmful. We have also worked hard to incorporate native plants and pollinator-friendly perennials throughout the farm, all of which provide a constant source of food for both day and night pollinators. We always turn to the most natural solutions for pest problems before trying any other methods. For example, every day from dawn to dusk, we have two of the sweetest ducks on constant slug patrol. We put up bat houses and take nightly enjoyment in watching the bats flit about in an acrobatic display through the mosquitos swarming our flowers. We adopted an old stray cat that befriended our boys, and she now serves as an excellent mouse deterrent. We plant tiny marigolds around all our pansies and roses, as they naturally deter the aphids. There are many things you can try for treating diseases and pests that have little to no adverse effect on anything beyond their target, and I highly encourage you to do so before resorting to something more aggressive.

It is essential to understand the more common adversaries of the pansy and viola and the options for treatment that are not harmful to all the delicate beings living among your flowers. When you must turn to a fungicide, I encourage you to try one that poses the least risk to the soil, other plants, and beneficial insects. Nowadays, you'll find many good products that are safe for organic gardening.

Example of leaf spot

ANTHRACNOSE AND LEAF SPOT

Anthracnose can present as pale yellow, brown, or gray spots, usually toward the edge of the leaves. As it progresses, the spots increase in size, often in a ring pattern, with the inside becoming dry and tan. Other types of leaf spot may show up in tan, brown, or black spots. They are all caused by varying types of fungus and must be treated accordingly. Leaf spot is seen most often in warm, wet months, as it is generally caused when water is splashed on the leaves and foliage from overhead watering or rainfall, creating the perfect environment for the fungus to thrive.

At the first sign of infection, remove all the affected leaves and treat the plants with a fungicide. I once had some pansies terribly affected by anthracnose. I treated them with a copper fungicide spray designed for organic gardening once a week for three weeks. I removed all the flowers and buds during those three weeks, and nearly all the plants recovered, except for a handful of severely infected ones that I had to remove and destroy.

POWDERY MILDEW

Powdery mildew is just as it sounds, a powdery white coating found on leaves and stems. It often presents in plants that are not receiving adequate air circulation.

Christianson's, a long-standing and reputable plant nursery located in the Skagit Valley of northwestern Washington, has graciously shared its recipe with the public for treating powdery mildew on roses, and I have found it also works very well on pansies. To make it, combine five gallons water, seven tablespoons baking soda, and a dash of liquid dish soap, mix well, and spray affected leaves thoroughly every two weeks or so.

ROOT ROT

Root rot stems from soilborne pathogens. The most common causes are overwatering or oversaturation of the roots for a long period or poor sanitation practices. While pansies need constant cool moisture deep at their root base, too much standing water will make them susceptible to rot. Symptoms first display as yellowing of the leaves or a purplish tint to the plant. Plants may also appear wilted or stunted, and when dug, the roots are black. Although some fungicides are effective in helping prevent root rot, once plants are infected, they must be removed and destroyed.

RUST

Rust tends to attack weaker plants in the wet season, although it always seems to take hold of my snapdragons even in their prime, regardless of weather and circumstance. It presents as reddish-brown spores on the underside of leaves, and it spreads very easily with wind and rain, as the spores are powdery and easy to knock loose. Immediately destroy any leaves showing signs of rust, and be sure to wash your hands thoroughly after handling infected foliage before you come in contact with any other plants. I use the same copper fungicide for treating rust that I use for treating anthracnose.

APHIDS

Like little vampires, these buggers cluster on the tips of leaves and stems, sucking out all the plant's sap. Additionally, their excretions drip down to other leaves and attract fungus. I have found that marigolds are a very successful deterrent, and I plant signet marigolds around my roses and pansies every year. I began doing this three seasons ago and have rarely seen an aphid on my pansies since. If you do find an infestation, one method is to spray the foliage with a firm current of water and remove the aphids by hand in the process. If this option makes you a bit squeamish, a spray of water mixed with a small amount of dish soap should also prove effective.

DEER

Deer love pansies. Maybe not as much as tender new leaves and buds on roses, but if pansies are available during their nightly foraging, chances are they will not pass them by. Living on the south end of an island, we have a large number of deer coming and going through our property and bedding down in our tree lines at night. The most effective method I have found to protect my plants from being gnawed by deer is a fence. I have all my most precious and tender plants fully fenced in so the deer cannot get to them. For plants and roses outside the fenced garden, I wrap them in a protective circle of chicken wire until the new delicate growth matures. Unfortunately, you cannot wrap pansies in chicken wire, but depending on the size and area where they are planted, you can encase them in a protective covering of chicken wire at night. Another option, which I have also had success with, is planting other plants around the pansies that deter the deer. Dill, mint, lavender, yarrow, larkspur, foxglove, poppies, peonies, and bee balm are all unappealing to deer. I have pansies growing in a bed with several roses, and by carpeting the entire area with lamb's ears (a member of the mint family), the deer have avoided both the pansies and the roses thus far.

SLUGS AND SNAILS

When it comes to pests of the pansy, there is none as persistent and incessant as the slug. These slimy creatures are especially threatening to seedlings and tender growth. I also feel like they have an uncanny ability to find the loveliest of all the flowers for their dining pleasure. Some options for natural methods to control slugs include wood ash, eggshells, and shade traps during the night, so you can locate and remove them by day. Persistent gardeners have been known to hunt slugs and snails at night, plucking them from the garden by hand. I am not one of them. My favorite means of slug control comes in the form of ducks, which I wholeheartedly recommend. On occasion, I employ Sluggo Plus to protect seedlings and new transplants. It is safe for organic gardening and uses iron phosphate, which occurs naturally in soil, making it safe for use around pets and wildlife.

SPIDER MITES

Spider mites tend to wreak havoc in warmer, drier months. As they are extremely small, you will notice the effects of their presence before you notice them. Yellow-mottled leaves will start to drop from the plant, and you may eventually see a fine webbing. Remove all infected leaves and wash the undersides of healthy leaves with soapy water. When completely dry, you can optionally dust leaves and soil with a gentle layer of weathered wood ash. Keeping soil evenly moist should help deter them, as they prefer very dry conditions.

Enemy number one, the slug

Ducks, the Protectors of Our Pansies

The western half of Washington and Oregon is like a treasure box in summer and truly an evergreen paradise. I'm told the area averages around 150 days of rain annually, and that feels about right. We have breathtaking mountains to the east, the crashing waves of the Pacific Ocean to the west, and a huge expanse of cedar and pine forests in between. We are also home to countless breathtaking lakes, an abundance of winding rivers, and some of the most pristine farmland in the country. While the summers can get hot and dry, there is usually ample moisture year-round that keeps the flora hydrated and lush. Even with the heat of summer, you will often find a layer of light dew on the grass in the early morning hours. Unfortunately, this also makes the Pacific Northwest a paradise for slugs.

As the number of pansies I grew increased year after year, the amount of time and effort I had to spend protecting them also increased. Pansies might be a slug's favorite flower, with bearded irises a close second. Which means I am now growing an abundance of the slug's two favorite flowers in an ever-misty and abundantly wet slug heaven. I had to find a way to keep one from the other, and it was going to take more than a few jugs of Sluggo Plus. I needed constant patrols. So, I got ducks.

We sourced our new charges from a farm that raises Muscovy ducks about an hour inland from our island. We read up on different breeds, and the Muscovy seemed like a good fit. We have two females, named Phlox and Honey. As soon as the sun comes up, the gate to their pen is opened, and they forage all day throughout the garden until returning to their shelter at dusk. They are incredibly tenacious in their efforts, and very rarely have my ducks disturbed or nibbled my actual flower crop, with the exception of some rose leaves.

While I cannot deny that ducks come with their own needs and costs, and there is no hiding the trail of unpleasantly splattered green poo that usually follows behind them, they are so worth the extra effort and cleanup on our little farm, as their role has been invaluable. There are so many fewer slugs in my pansy beds, and my irises have benefited significantly as well. In addition, it just makes me really happy to have their company when I'm out working among the flowers. I personally cannot recommend them highly enough, as we absolutely love our ducks, and they have truly excelled in their role of protectors of our pansies.

Our duck, Phlox, who is on constant slug patrol

Embracing Difficult Seasons with Pansies and Violas

I have found it is always better to work with nature rather than against it. Sometimes that means turning a difficult situation in your favor by pivoting and increasing your workload to prevent loss. It can also mean stepping back and accepting that, in some cases, rest and release are the best way forward. Each season seems to bring with it more exceptions than the last. The common rules of nature are being stretched, bent, and even broken as the climate shifts and the Earth responds accordingly.

The last few seasons have proven some of the most challenging for growing flowers here in the Pacific Northwest. In 2021, we experienced a "heat dome" in late June that lasted almost a week. Temperatures peaked at 118°F (48°C), which is almost forty degrees (twenty-three degrees) higher than our normal temperatures at that time of year. My cosmos looked like they had been baked on a cookie sheet in the oven. The roses bloomed in shades I had never seen before or since. And the pansies? Well, the pansies persisted. They persevered through the hottest temperatures we have ever experienced and continued to bloom throughout the rest of that summer.

In 2022, we set a record for the driest summer. On average, Seattle sees about 3 inches (7.5 cm) of rainfall between the end of June and the end of September, but we received only a half inch (12 mm) in 2022. We also saw the most days above 90°F (32°C) that we have ever seen. Plus, that summer followed the third coldest and tenth wettest April on record. There were multiple times that year that I wanted to give up on growing flowers for the season. The pansies, however, persevered, just as they had the year before. Pansies, like people, can weather incredibly difficult circumstances if careful and intentional preparations are made to allow them to do so.

Back in 2017, I decided I was going to run my first marathon, and I was terrified of a DNF (did not finish). I have always been a slow runner, so it was never about the time. I just wanted to complete it. I was deeply devoted to my training for an entire year. I knew that preparing my body as best I could was the only chance I had to accomplish that distance. I couldn't afford to miss a single training run, so I invested in all-weather gear to guarantee I did every run, regardless of temperature and precipitation. I fueled my body with foods that made it function efficiently and kept it well hydrated at all times. I made sure I had plenty of sleep and spent time stretching and rolling out sore muscles so I could give my body the best chance of recovery without injury. As the months went on, my pace improved and my body recovered more quickly. By the time the marathon arrived, I was ready because I had given my body everything it needed to accomplish what I was asking of it.

Leaf spot on pansies

The following year, I backed off my training significantly, more or less returning to my normal routine. On a whim, I decided to run a half marathon. I thought, how out of shape can I be? The difference was immense. Not only was it much more difficult and my pace slower, but my recovery took considerably longer. If exceptional demands continue to be present, exceptional care must continue to be taken.

In those two atypical growing seasons of 2021 and 2022, I decided that I needed to care for my flowers the same way I cared for my body when something extraordinary was being asked of it. When not running a marathon, when just maintaining good health, my daily habits do not have to be stringent. Just as a normal growing season, with expected amounts of rainfall and moderate temperatures, doesn't require abnormal levels of diligence. The flowers still need to be watered, fed, and weeded, but these are daily tasks that are easily managed and anticipated every season. But when the summer temperatures soar and the rain doesn't fall, the flowers need exceptional preparations and recovery. A difficult season is a flower's marathon.

In both 2021 and 2022, I took extra steps in caring for the pansies and violas. I made sure to water them more often, slowly and for long periods, so there was always water deep at their roots at least 4 to 6 inches (10 to 15 cm) below the surface. I was relentless in my deadheading to ensure they pushed as much energy as possible into their roots and foliage. Twice a month, I removed all the buds and flowers. I made sure they were fed weekly, and I kept their beds well weeded to prevent any competition for nutrients. While almost all these tasks are required even during a normal season, I modified them accordingly for the extra demands placed on the plants by the excessive heat and abnormally dry growing conditions. Had I not given the pansies and violas what they needed to replenish after what they had endured, they would have likely perished—a DNF in their own little marathon, if you will.

Heat and drought are not the only components that can make for a difficult season. An overly wet season can cause just as much trouble as an overly dry one. With moisture often come disease and mildew. Foliage tends to suffer when water pools on leaves and at roots. I have found the best defense against a wet spring or summer is well-prepared soil with good drainage. Alternatively, if you have the means, you can grow your pansies and violas in caterpillar tunnels or high tunnels. This allows their foliage to stay dry, and watering can be accomplished and well controlled through irrigation. Just be sure the plants have plenty of airflow and the tunnels are properly vented, especially when the temperature climbs.

The other culprits with the potential to ruin an entire season's pansy crop are pests, be it insects or animals. I have had deer eat the new growth off every available rose, and I have had rabbits eat every single stem of phlox. This past season brought a new challenge when mice decided to take up residence in one of my pansy beds. Living on the south end of an island well inhabited by wildlife, we have accepted the abundance of unwanted visitors that pop in and out of the flowers, but we have never had them permanently move into the flower beds. We are very careful to allow wildlife their own space, and we do not bait or poison mice, as that poses great harm to the many birds of prey who call the trees on and around our property home. We try to control pests by encouraging natural predators to reside more frequently near the garden. While the mice did not eat the pansies, they disturbed the roots and were killing them off slowly but surely. In this situation, for our farm, the best course of action was no action. I resigned that bed to the mice for the rest of the summer. Come fall, we dug up the bed and replaced all the soil. I still had plenty of pansies growing in other locations, so only a small portion of my crop was lost. I have found this is a very useful strategy when you have pests and ample fauna. Planting in multiple sites also decreases the chance of an entire crop being infected with disease.

Difficult seasons are likely going to be more frequent than ideal ones. I encourage you, as I do myself, to pick your battles accordingly. When it's in your control to do something about it, gather your fortitude and put in the work. But when nature has dealt you a hand you probably cannot win, fold your cards with peace and let yourself exhale. One of the best things about growing flowers is that as long as there are springs, there are opportunities to try again: to do it differently because it didn't work, or do it the same way because it did and it was amazing.

As for the flowers themselves, the pansies and violas that may be less than perfect with their nibbled petals, spotted leaves, smaller-than-normal bloom, or perhaps even a shade off in color due to excessive temperatures, I encourage you to look upon them with grace. They don't have to be perfect to be celebrated. They can still fill a vase and light up a room. Their ability to inspire joy is no less just because they are blemished. Difficult seasons take a toll on both flowers and growers, but there is something extra beautiful in overcoming adversity. There are plenty of uses for less-than-perfect pansies, especially considering they are an edible flower. In fact, if there is any flower that can still be made useful after a difficult season, it is the pansy.

Pansies are much more hardy and resilient than they've been given credit for these past several decades.

CHAPTER 3

Exceptional Pansies and Violas in Cultivation Today

During my ongoing search for the pansy's curiously hidden history, I simultaneously contemplated its place among well-known flowers today. It is not a large, showy flower like the peony or the dahlia, nor does it command the size and space of the rose or iris. Nonetheless, I think it is just as exquisite and equally varied in colors and patterns as its counterparts.

Unlike the short flowering window of peonies and irises, pansies and violas bloom from early spring into fall, withstanding frosts and even winter in some growing zones. If proper care and methods are employed, there isn't a month of the year they can't be grown in temperate climates. They can also be cultivated in containers and pots, making them an ideal option for windows, terraces, porches, and rooftops. While it is possible to grow roses, peonies, and dahlias this way, the pots must be quite large and require significant space, while the easygoing pansy does well in both small pots and large containers. The pansy does not require a trellis or corralling, nor do the stems need to be staked, and it tolerates some shade. It is a flower that is accessible to anyone and everyone, grand garden or not. Its broad usefulness has been forgotten, and its full potential has gone untapped for far too long. Despite being overshadowed, the pansy has persevered like no other flower, both figuratively and literally.

Every thirty to forty years, attempts have been made to give this flower the full recognition it deserves, but it seems to have receded once again into the strict classification of low-level seasonal landscaping, with no other suitable use considered. This is not to say that it shouldn't remain a top pick for beds and borders. It has achieved this standing for good reason.

A vase of Italian pansies commands center stage.

Pansies can be sown in fall to flower in early spring, adding color and texture to otherwise bare areas of the garden. Few better options exist to fill the gap of color after the daffodils and tulips have ceased. They continue prolifically through May and June, when the irises and peonies have finished but the bulk of the annuals have not yet come into bloom. If sown in early summer, pansies will come into their first flush in fall when other flowers have already gone dormant. Pansies and violas are exceptional in landscaping, and while it's important they be seen for their other virtues, it by no means detracts from their superior usefulness in this area. I am a proponent of pansies being grown in all ways, all places, and for all purposes.

If you are wondering about the comparison to roses, peonies, irises, and dahlias, which are known for their usefulness in arrangements as cut flowers, it is because I know the pansy to be useful in the same way. While flowers are all about personal preference, and each person has a different idea of what constitutes a perfect bouquet, for me there is nothing better than a vase full of long-stemmed pansies.

The varieties I grow for cut flowers are usually different from most varieties found at home and garden stores. I grow all my pansies from seed, as I have found this is the best way to achieve the most significant stem length. It's also how I have been able to acquire the most beautiful varieties available today. That said, it has more often than not been quite a struggle to find sources for the varieties I most want to grow. Seed suppliers work off of supply and demand, and until there is more definitive demand for these rarer colors and patterns, they will not be readily available. This is something I am hoping you and I can change.

I want to see more pansies reminiscent of the varieties lost so many decades ago. Substantial opportunity exists for new varieties to be hybridized just as they were in the mid-nineteenth century. With enough demand, we can hopefully encourage further seed production and regain ease of access to the varieties that are currently so hard for small growers and hobby gardeners to source. With continued dedication, we can introduce varieties similar to those lost, while simultaneously bringing about new shades and styles capable of shifting with modern trends. The pansy is the one flower that can effortlessly bridge nostalgia and sentiment with the demands of present-day floristry, and I believe now is the time to see this flower back in the spotlight.

I will be continuing my trials of one hundred or so varieties every year in an ongoing effort to discover and share those that I have found to possess the best fragrance, most exquisite colors, and greatest reliability as a cut flower. I must disclose that I do not show flowers, nor am I personally interested in perfect specimens. It is often the aberrant blooms that I find most alluring and exquisite. I am simply a modest grower who became unexpectedly and wholly passionate about these underrated little flowers and look forward to a future filled with them.

There are a few dozen varieties I have grown to love the most. Whether it is their color, shape, fragrance, or performance that earned my devotion, I hope you will consider growing some of them yourself. I have noted both their average height when grown traditionally and their potential stem length when grown specifically for cut flowers.

If you are already an avid grower, I hope you'll find at least one new variety that further deepens your love of the pansy.

For the florists, I encourage you to tap into the incredible presence these pansies can bring to modern bouquets and arrangements.

For the artists, the texture and color of these varieties are exquisite inspiration, and their little faces are just imploring you to paint them.

An incredibly beautiful example of a self-sown mystery viola

'Ballerina'

SPECIES
Viola ×wittrockiana

BLOOM SIZE
Medium, 1¼ to 2 inches
(3 to 5 cm)

HEIGHT
10 inches (25 cm)

CUTTING STEM LENGTH
16 inches (40 cm)

FRAGRANCE
Mild

COLOR
Mulberry, eggplant, violet,
gold, cream, honey, rose

A far cry from the pansies that graced exhibition halls a century and a half ago, 'Ballerina' is one of several heavily ruffled varieties that are available to growers today. Completely free in form, the petals flutter and flounce like a ballerina's tutu. The edges are crimped, rumpled, gathered, and crinkled, lending to varied shapes in every bloom.

'Ballerina' blooms in a wide range of colors, from deep burgundy to mulberry, violet to eggplant purple, mauve to rose pink, and lemon to honey gold. Many blooms have a soft cream face behind a heavily veined blotch, as if the blotch itself was applied in watercolor and bled across the petals in little inky tributaries.

'Bunny Ears'

This is possibly the sweetest variety I have ever grown. When you hear talk of how endearing the faces of pansies can be, this is exactly it. The top two petals are elongated and narrow, giving the appearance of little bunny ears. Blooms are in shades of magenta pink to orchid purple, with deep purple whiskers and a little golden eye gazing back at you from the milky white face on the lower petals.

I have filled countless terra-cotta pots with 'Bunny Ears' and have now begun to plant it en masse around all my perennials. It is one of the more fragrant varieties, making it an ideal option for sitting areas and entryways. I have not been able to achieve stems any longer than 12 inches (30 cm), but it is still lovely in smaller vases. I've seen it listed as both *Viola ×wittrockiana* and *V. cornuta* in multiple reputable sources, so I cannot say for certain which is correct. I can say that it very much resembles the original *V. cornuta* in form.

SPECIES
Viola ×wittrockiana
or *V. cornuta*

BLOOM SIZE
Small, ¾ to 1½ inches
(2 to 4 cm)

HEIGHT
8 inches (20 cm)

CUTTING STEM LENGTH
12 inches (30 cm)

FRAGRANCE
Strong

COLOR
Magenta pink, orchid
purple, white

'Can Can'

SPECIES
Viola ×wittrockiana

BLOOM SIZE
Medium, 1½ to 2½ inches
(4 to 6 cm)

HEIGHT
10 inches (25 cm)

CUTTING STEM LENGTH
20 inches (50 cm)

FRAGRANCE
Moderate

COLOR
Rich red, violet purple,
lemon to golden yellow,
soft to deep pink, white

Several varieties of ruffled pansies are available right now that are amazingly lovely both in the garden and in the vase, and this is one of them. Just as countless ruffles swirl about creating a rainbowed blur on the stages of darkened Paris, so do the ruffles in the broad spectrum of color found within 'Can Can'.

The vibrant hues found in this mix range from claret red to plum purple, lemon yellow to sun-ripened peach, and pure white to buttery cream. Some have blotches, some have whiskers, and several shades of color are often found in a single bloom. The variance is remarkably diverse, and the ruffles are some of the most substantial, making this variety an exceptional choice for a dramatic spot of bright color. The richness seems to be further enhanced by cooler temperatures, and the lush green foliage appears a bit more resistant to leaf spot than other similar varieties.

'Chianti Mix'

Possibly the most sought-after pansy at this time for arrangements, the ruffled, silky petals of this seed mix boast countless romantic shades, from crimson, carmine, mauve, and cherry to raspberry, rose, peach, honey, and lemon cream. Complementary streaks and splashes of contrast on each petal ensure no two flowers are alike. With a mild fragrance and willowy long stems, it has a strong presence in bouquets. Its bloom size also means it can be a focal flower on its own.

Thankfully, the strict guidelines for show pansies are no longer determining the course of propagation, so we are able to revel in the beautiful relaxed shapes and colors of 'Chianti Mix'. While in the past a pansy was considered inferior if its eye lacked a clear cut, varieties like 'Chianti Mix' demonstrate that a gently fading eye across the lower petal is nothing to be shunned. With its incredible variation in both color and shape, this variety is easily one of my favorites. I tend to pair it with roses, bearded irises, and phlox, as the colors and ruffles are timelessly elegant.

SPECIES
Viola ×wittrockiana

BLOOM SIZE
Medium, 1¼ to 2 inches
(3 to 5 cm)

HEIGHT
8 inches (20 cm)

CUTTING STEM LENGTH
20 inches (50 cm)

FRAGRANCE
Mild

COLOR
Crimson, mauve, rose, peach, lemon cream

Delta 'Pink Shades'

SPECIES
Viola ×wittrockiana

BLOOM SIZE
Large, 2½ to 3 inches
(6 to 7.5 cm)

HEIGHT
6 inches (15 cm)

CUTTING STEM LENGTH
10 inches (25 cm)

FRAGRANCE
None detected

COLOR
Graduated shades of
palest pink to deep rose

From the palest of shell to the deepest rose, there are many color variations in this variety. You will find cherry blossom pink with a deep violet blotch, cotton candy pink with a face washed in lilac, ballerina pink with deep eggplant whiskers, and orchid rose in a rippled reflection of tones fading and gathering throughout the petals. Some flowers bloom in such a delicate light pink that they appear almost white. This is a very romantic variety, and if you are looking to add some pink to your garden, this would be my top pick.

When growing pansies for cut flowers, the larger bloom varieties are not usually recommended. The petals flop over, for one, and the stems rarely get long enough to fill anything other than a very small jar. Most of the varieties with an especially large bloom size have been bred for decades to remain compact and resist elongating. The Delta series is one of the few varieties I have found that can still, on occasion, be used as a cut flower.

Delta 'Pure Light Blue'

Few flowers bloom in shades of true blue. Luckily, pansies are one of them. The Delta series is very popular among growers for both habit and color. Several shades of the series will often be stocked at local nurseries and home garden stores, particularly because of the large bloom size. I have trialed several pansies in the clan, and the Delta 'Pure Light Blue' is one of my favorites. Two additional factors have contributed to the popularity of this series: its consistent output of flowers and an ability to tolerate longer periods of shade without affecting its bloom window.

While the outer petals are pale icy blue, the color intensifies toward the center of the bloom, often to include the veining, giving it an elegant presence. It adds a beautiful splash of color to small bouquets and arrangements. Although it lacks fragrance, its ability to tolerate cold makes it a great option for spring flowering. Climates with mild seasons may see it flower in winter.

SPECIES
Viola ×wittrockiana

BLOOM SIZE
Large, 2½ to 3 inches
(6 to 7.5 cm)

HEIGHT
6 inches (15 cm)

CUTTING STEM LENGTH
10 inches (25 cm)

FRAGRANCE
None detected

COLOR
Graduated pale to dark
blue or lavender

'Envy'

SPECIES
Viola ×wittrockiana

BLOOM SIZE
Medium, 1½ to 2½ inches
(4 to 6 cm)

HEIGHT
12 inches (30 cm)

CUTTING STEM LENGTH
20 inches (50 cm)

FRAGRANCE
Mild

COLOR
Unique shades of olive
green, old gold, and
purple

Featuring one of the most astonishing colors of any flower I have ever grown, 'Envy' is easily one of my top ten picks for pansies. It tends to open in rich antiqued gold before taking on an olive sheen. There are definite underlying tones of intense purple that can come through stronger, depending on the temperatures. As it ages, it turns almost sepia bronze, looking as though it is suspended in time.

I love using this one in arrangements, as it adds such an unexpected bit of magic to any bouquet work. It perfectly complements the deep purple of the 'Ebb Tide' rose and also blends with the unique palette of 'Koko Loko' and 'Honey Dijon'. I am particularly fond of pairing it with deep red roses as well, like 'Hot Cocoa' and 'Munstead Wood'. When used in floral work, this pansy is limited only by the imagination of the arranger.

'Envy' is, unfortunately, quite infamous for low germination. I have trialed it from several sources, all with the same results. That said, I have had several plants of 'Envy' overwinter with no protection, and once the variety gets going, it is very floriferous. Despite the initial frustration, it is definitely a variety worth growing. A little extra effort in sowing additional seed will compensate for the low germination rates.

Flamenco 'Soft Light Azure Limonette'

SPECIES
Viola ×wittrockiana

BLOOM SIZE
Medium, 1¼ to 2 inches
(3 to 5 cm)

HEIGHT
10 inches (25 cm)

CUTTING STEM LENGTH
20 inches (50 cm)

FRAGRANCE
Mild

COLOR
Pale lavender, lilac, pink

This is a newer variety for me, and to be honest, I wasn't expecting much when I ordered the seeds. I think I was more intrigued by the lengthy name than the sample photo in the catalog. Don't you just love when flowers exceed your expectations? I was truly taken aback with how beautiful this variety is in person and how much I loved it once it bloomed. It has earned itself permanent residence in my garden for as long as I am able to source seeds.

Most of the flowers bloom in pale shades of lavender and lilac, but some open in cherry-blossom pink, and others are very near white. They are sufficiently ruffled and incredibly romantic, and each bloom seems to have delicate details all its own. From a carefully traced border around every petal a few shades darker than the bloom itself to pronounced whiskers and veining, they are the flower you would imagine a garden fairy using to craft her spring salutation gown.

Flamenco 'Terracotta'

Since I first started trialing pansies, my long-standing favorite variety has been 'Chianti Mix' (see page 103). The ruffles, the colors, the patterns of streaking and veining—there really was no other variety I grew that could match its elegance, until now.

Flamenco 'Terracotta' is a slightly larger, slightly more fragrant, slightly more ruffled, and slightly more artistic version of 'Chianti'. They are quite similar in palette and even pattern, but I have found that the exceptional blooms I look for in the 'Chianti Mix' are more common in Flamenco 'Terracotta'.

These flowers bloom in shades of soft honey, pale peach, blush pink, fresh cream, and occasionally sorceress purple. What makes them truly exceptional, though, is that on the soft shades of canvassed petals, bold streaks of raspberry, claret, dusky mauve, and deep apricot are brushed with abandon. Many of the flowers have intricate veining in both complementary and contrasting colors. It is a truly wondrous variety.

SPECIES
Viola ×wittrockiana

BLOOM SIZE
Medium, 1¾ to 2½ inches (4.5 to 6 cm)

HEIGHT
10 inches (25 cm)

CUTTING STEM LENGTH
20 inches (50 cm)

FRAGRANCE
Moderate

COLOR
Wildly varied with multiple shades of cream, blush pink, apricot, honey, lavender, and raspberry, often together on one flower

Flamenco 'Tricolour Rose'

SPECIES
Viola ×wittrockiana

BLOOM SIZE
Medium, 1¼ to 2¼ inches
(3 to 5.5 cm)

HEIGHT
10 inches (25 cm)

CUTTING STEM LENGTH
20 inches (50 cm)

FRAGRANCE
Mild

COLOR
Raspberry to carmine
pink, mauve to burgundy,
eggplant purple to pale
lavender

Shades of crushed raspberry, garden-rose pink, rich burgundy, and pale lavender fill the petals of Flamenco 'Tricolour Rose'. Almost all the flowers bloom with a blotch of deep eggplant purple, and many of the ruffled petals are etched in frothy white.

This variety easily catches the eye from across the garden. I recommend planting it among the roses or at the base of sweet peas, as it serves as a lovely companion to every shade of white, cream, pink, or purple.

As part of the Flamenco series, it is equivalent in size to 'Soft Light Azure Limonette' (see page 110) and a bit smaller than 'Terracotta' (see page 113). The ruffles are consistently present in every flower. While looking over all the pansies in bloom as I make selections for cutting, I am often drawn to this one. It really does stand out.

'Floral Days Morning Dew'

Pansies and violas possess such a unique fragrance. It is not intensely sweet like the violet, but more delectable—like standing in the shop of a chocolatier with your eyes closed and gently inhaling the creamy scent that swirls around you. I've heard others say they smell like almonds, but I stand firm that they smell like chocolate. Some varieties have an ever-so-faint hint of this scent, and others are so fragrant they can fill a room. This variety is one of the most fragrant.

In shades of lemon, strawberry, peach, and plum, they feel like summer on a stem. A bit smaller than many of their kin but well varied in color, they make a beautiful gathering all their own in a petite vase. Many have vivid whiskers, lending to that legendary sweet face the pansy is known for.

Because the flowers are so wonderfully fragrant, this variety makes an excellent option for pots and containers.

SPECIES
Viola ×wittrockiana

BLOOM SIZE
Small, 1¼ to 1½ inches
(3 to 4 cm)

HEIGHT
8 inches (20 cm)

CUTTING STEM LENGTH
14 inches (35.5 cm)

FRAGRANCE
Strong

COLOR
Raspberry, lemon, peach,
plum

Frizzle Sizzle 'Lemonberry'

SPECIES
Viola ×wittrockiana

BLOOM SIZE
Large, 2 to 2½ inches
(5 to 6 cm)

HEIGHT
8 inches (20 cm)

CUTTING STEM LENGTH
14 inches (35.5 cm)

FRAGRANCE
Moderate

COLOR
Lemon to honey yellow,
violet, magenta, and
eggplant purple, with
cream highlights

Yellow and purple together are not a combination I normally seek out. But ask me again in several years, and it might be my favorite. Palettes are ever evolving, and personal preference is subject to change through the passing seasons and years. That said, every once in a while, a flower comes along that manages to present an unlikely blend of colors in a way that cannot be described as anything other than perfectly achieved. That is how I see Frizzle Sizzle 'Lemonberry'.

More frost tolerant than many, this is an exceptional option for bedding and borders. Additionally, the color combination and striking blotches, whiskers, and veining that present from bloom to bloom make it well placed in pots and containers where it can be closely admired. The ruffled petals give it an ever-changing shape as it opens, and the more I grow this variety, the more joy I find in it.

Frizzle Sizzle 'Orange'

I am especially fond of several shades of orange in flowers—peach, apricot, pumpkin, and burnt orange, to name a few. I grow an abundance of orange-shaded dahlias and roses every year. But I am not normally drawn to brighter shades of orange, such as tangerine, papaya, or mango. Frizzle Sizzle 'Orange' is the exception.

I first saw this variety at a nursery. A dear friend and I both spotted it from quite a ways away and involuntarily squealed in unison, as the little orange ruffles were like sparkling gems on that rainy morning. I have grown several varieties from this series and love the frilly flounced petals. This brighter orange was a step outside my normal preferences, but it is so striking, I adored it instantly. If you love orange, which I'm finding more and more people do nowadays, this is an excellent option.

SPECIES
Viola ×wittrockiana

BLOOM SIZE
Large, 2 to 2½ inches
(5 to 6 cm)

HEIGHT
8 inches (20 cm)

CUTTING STEM LENGTH
14 inches (35.5 cm)

FRAGRANCE
Mild

COLOR
Tangerine orange

Frizzle Sizzle 'Raspberry'

SPECIES
Viola ×wittrockiana

BLOOM SIZE
Large, 2 to 2½ inches
(5 to 6 cm)

HEIGHT
8 inches (20 cm)

CUTTING STEM LENGTH
14 inches (35.5 cm)

FRAGRANCE
Moderate

COLOR
Eggplant purple, milk
white, lemon cream

Frizzle Sizzle 'Raspberry', the third variety I'm including from the Frizzle Sizzle series, is everything delectable and beguiling. Some varieties prompt imaginings of desserts, and this is one of them. It makes me think of a warm berry pie with vanilla ice cream.

The upper petals are a consistent eggplant to plum, with a blotched face to match. The eye is a steady gold, and little stretched traces of berry-colored rays extend beyond the blotch. The blotch rests on petals of white, some like fresh milk and others rich cream with a hint of lemon zest. Occasionally, the lower petals will be entirely encircled in purple.

This is a wonderful variety for use with white, pink, and lavender roses, as the shades so perfectly complement them.

Imperial 'Antique Shades'

Faded salmon pink, smoky apricot, spring yellow, and fresh cream on large, soft petals make Imperial 'Antique Shades' one of the most beautiful choices for pastel shades in the flower garden.

The large bloom and long stem also make it a top pick when growing for cutting. Luckily, the seed for this variety is becoming more readily available. It pairs beautifully with early spring flowers like daffodils and hyacinths, but I especially love it with garden roses. It is also a perfect companion for dahlias, many of which bloom in the same shades of blush, peach, and honey.

This variety is particularly susceptible to root rot and leaf spot if prolonged oversaturation occurs, so you will need to monitor it closely.

SPECIES
Viola ×wittrockiana

BLOOM SIZE
Large, 2 to 3 inches
(5 to 7.5 cm)

HEIGHT
8 inches (20 cm)

CUTTING STEM LENGTH
20 inches (50 cm)

FRAGRANCE
Moderate

COLOR
Rose pink, lemon to honey yellow, apricot, cream

Inspire 'Peach Shades'

From pure ivory with splashes of lemon and orange zest near the eye to the palest of blush with streaks of pumpkin, this stylish pansy brings to mind a Champagne sunset. You will find faded raspberry with a touch of tangerine as well as the softest butter yellow paired with a dollop of warm apricot. While there are extensive varieties of pansies in shades of reds, purples, and yellows, there are only a few in the unique palette of Inspire 'Peach Shades'.

The colors are highly romantic and strongly hint to citrus near the eye of every bloom, making it perfect for summer wedding work. Garden roses, irises, and peonies are its ideal partners in bouquets and arrangements. Because Inspire 'Peach Shades' is a larger bloom, it maintains a steadfast presence, rather than getting lost among the filler flowers and greenery.

This one holds a place in my ten favorite varieties. I use it often in bouquets and have filled the rose beds near the front of my home with it.

SPECIES
Viola ×wittrockiana

BLOOM SIZE
Large, 2 to 3 inches
(5 to 7.5 cm)

HEIGHT
8 inches (20 cm)

CUTTING STEM LENGTH
12 inches (30 cm)

FRAGRANCE
Mild

COLOR
Blush to raspberry pink, pale peach to warm apricot, ivory to cream

Magnum 'Lilac Shades'

SPECIES
Viola ×wittrockiana

BLOOM SIZE
Large, 3 to 3¼ inches
(7.5 to 8 cm)

HEIGHT
6 inches (15 cm)

CUTTING STEM LENGTH
12 inches (30 cm)

FRAGRANCE
None detected

COLOR
Lilac to lavender

The Magnum series is another popular choice among growers who enjoy a larger bloom size. I have grown several varieties in the series, and I have found 'Lilac Shades' to be one of the best.

From the palest of amethyst to lavender, this variety looks to be the work of a watercolorist, with the paint gently washed over alabaster-white petals, concentrating through the veining, and pooling at the edges in lapping waves of heather. Some flowers bloom in such a delicate light purple that they appear almost white. The rays look burgundy near the golden eye but deepen to eggplant as they reach across the petals. This is a very romantic variety, and if you are looking to add some of the softest violet purple to your garden, this would be a great pick.

Matrix 'Coastal Sunrise Mix'

SPECIES
Viola ×wittrockiana

BLOOM SIZE
Extra large, 3 to 3½ inches
(7.5 to 9 cm)

HEIGHT
8 inches

CUTTING STEM LENGTH
Not suitable for long-stem
cutting

FRAGRANCE
Mild

COLOR
Blue, mauve, rose, yellow

These are the largest pansies I have ever grown. They definitely stand out in the garden, and this particular mix has a nice array of color. The Matrix series is said to do best during the long, drawn-out days of late summer and early fall when the temperatures linger on the warmer side. They are also reputed to have the most flowers per plant of all larger pansies, making them a great option for beds and borders.

Just as the name suggests, these pansies bloom in all the colors found in a coastal sunrise. Some are a vivid blue purple, like the ocean when daylight hasn't yet fully illuminated it. Many have a warm bright yellow halo, like gentle sunlight, encircling the dark blotch that appears on every flower. Shades of raspberry, mauve, and rose saturate the petals of the remaining blooms. When gathered together, they have the makings of a lovely sunrise in flower form.

This is a wonderful variety for use in living wreaths.

'Moulin Rouge'

When it comes to heavily ruffled pansies, 'Moulin Rouge' tends to demand center stage. This beautiful Italian variety is similar to cousins 'Can Can' (see page 100) and 'Ballerina' (see page 96), each with its own slight variation in pattern, color, and form. I have found 'Moulin Rouge' and 'Can Can' to have a more generous bloom size than 'Ballerina', but if you enjoy growing any one of them, chances are you will adore growing all of them.

While 'Can Can' has been a bit more vibrant in the majority of its blooms, 'Moulin Rouge' has put forth some absolutely ethereal shades of celestial blue throughout the season, in addition to tones of crimson, plum, topaz, and mauve. Ranging from gentle flutters on the edges to intensely ruffled throughout, it's definitely a showy variety and worthy of being a focal flower all its own.

SPECIES
Viola ×wittrockiana

BLOOM SIZE
Medium, 1½ to 2½ inches (4 to 6 cm)

HEIGHT
10 inches (25 cm)

CUTTING STEM LENGTH
20 inches (50 cm)

FRAGRANCE
Moderate

COLOR
Crimson to plum, topaz to caramel, celestial blue to puce, mauve to salmon

Nature 'Antique Shades'

SPECIES
Viola ×wittrockiana

BLOOM SIZE
Small, 1¼ to 1¾ inches
(3 to 4.5 cm)

HEIGHT
10 inches (25 cm)

CUTTING STEM LENGTH
16 inches (40 cm)

FRAGRANCE
Mild

COLOR
Raspberry, gold, cream,
blush, apricot

The Nature series has some beautiful colors available, and this is one of the best. Somewhat reminiscent of the 'Antique Shades' found in the Imperial series (see page 125), it has a daintier bloom size more closely resembling the original heartsease over the modern garden pansy. The stems are long enough for bouquet work, and the blooms add nice bits of color to spring and summer arrangements. This is a popular variety for beds and beneath roses, as the colors are in the palette of a midsummer sunrise. One of the easier varieties with reliable germination to find seed for, it's a great choice if you want to start growing pansies from seed in this color range.

While some flowers will come in deep raspberry, most bloom in pale lemon meringue, warm apricot, pumpkin cake, strawberry lemonade, and cotton candy. They gently fade like antique silk ribbon, and their sepia-brown whiskers give them a truly timeless grace. Lightly fragrant and typically vigorous, they are all around a really wonderful addition to any garden or pot.

Nature 'Mulberry Shades'

Of the several varieties I have grown in the Nature series, I have not been disappointed in any of them. My favorites are merited because of my color preference, not because one performed any better than the next. While 'Antique Shades' (see page 134) is a variety I will confidently grow for many years, if I had to choose only from this series, it might actually be 'Mulberry Shades'.

I have yet to find another pansy comparable in color to 'Mulberry Shades'. It is unbelievably rich and intoxicating without being garish or gaudy. The hues displayed throughout bring to mind the Tuscan countryside, desert sunsets, and terra-cotta pots sprawling across crackled sienna clay dirt. Shades of rich berry pie and mulled cider are also found among its flowers. It is everything warm and smoldering, and letting your eyes linger on a vase of 'Mulberry Shades' as you drift off to sleep provides the same entrancing calm as watching embers in a dying fire. The colors really must be seen in person to understand their full allure.

SPECIES
Viola ×wittrockiana

BLOOM SIZE
Small, 1¼ to 1¾ inches
(3 to 4.5 cm)

HEIGHT
10 inches (25 cm)

CUTTING STEM LENGTH
20 inches (50 cm)

FRAGRANCE
Moderate

COLOR
Garnet, cinnamon, copper, caramel, pumpkin, smoky plum

'Pandora's Box'

SPECIES
Viola ×wittrockiana

BLOOM SIZE
Medium, 1¼ to 2 inches
(3 to 5 cm)

HEIGHT
12 inches (30 cm)

CUTTING STEM LENGTH
16 inches (40 cm)

FRAGRANCE
Mild

COLOR
Strawberry punch,
apricot, lavender, lemon
cream, pale violet

In a palette of soft colors that don't feel aged or antiquated, 'Pandora's Box' is everything fresh and full of late spring and early summer. It's reliably floriferous throughout the season, and I've had several visitors so drawn to it that they make a point to ask where to buy the seed. The bloom size is small to medium, and the shape is slightly more rounded than is typical, making it reminiscent of the original *Viola lutea*.

The colors seem to shift a bit with the temperature, and the entire mix reminds me of berries, custards, and all the best summertime desserts. Thoughts of fresh cream, strawberry shortcake, raspberry mousse, and lemon pie will fill your mind on seeing this delectable and tempting array, which, being edible, is perfect for use in baking and garnishing.

'Pandora Flambé'

Pandora 'Flambé' was quite a surprise this past season. I gave it a try as I had really come to love the mix found in 'Pandora's Box' (see page 138). I expected this one to be similar to the Sorbet 'Honeybee' viola (see page 173) in color and pattern, a flower of which I am particularly fond. But when 'Pandora Flambe' first bloomed, I found it completely underwhelming. The colors didn't wow me. It was just kind of there. But then it shifted . . .

What it lacks in the opening act, it more than makes up for over the duration of its flowering, but most especially of all, in its finale. The colors go through this marvelous transformation of metallic intensity, and it seems as though you can actually see the veining turn from a light rust to deep mahogany as it fades, with a pellucid copper overlay on honey-caramel petals. Certainly not what I was expecting from this variety, and I am so glad I gave it a go.

SPECIES
Viola ×wittrockiana

BLOOM SIZE
Medium, 1¼ to 2 inches
(3 to 5 cm)

HEIGHT
12 inches (30 cm)

CUTTING STEM LENGTH
16 inches (40 cm)

FRAGRANCE
Mild

COLOR
Cinnamon, caramel,
copper, bronze,
mahogany, rust

'Plums and Peaches'

SPECIES
Viola ×wittrockiana

BLOOM SIZE
Small, 1 to 1½ inches
(2.5 to 4 cm)

HEIGHT
10 inches (25 cm)

CUTTING STEM LENGTH
14 inches (35.5 cm)

FRAGRANCE
Mild

COLOR
Peach, caramel, honey,
plum, lilac, mauve

One of the varieties that most resembles the ornamentation of watercolor, 'Plums and Peaches' (or 'Peaches and Plums', depending on the source) is a truly refined little gem among pansies.

Similar to the palette of 'Pandora's Box' (see page 138), it has beautiful shades of summer sunshine and ripe berries. Within this variety, you will find apricot petals lovingly painted with strokes of smoky plum, petals the color of fresh linen streaked with ripe blackberry, and flowers that look like peach cobbler dripping with blueberry syrup and a dollop of fresh cream. The amethyst whiskers lend the most agreeable expression on their gentle faces. I adore this variety, and if you happen to be cultivating a fairy garden, this would be a most welcome addition.

'Rococo'

Gently fluttering petals and contrasting colors set 'Rococo' apart from other pansies of similar habit. Although not as heavily ruffled as the dancing ladies—'Ballerina', 'Can Can', and 'Moulin Rouge' (pages 96, 100, and 133, respectively)—it still has enough frill to garner fair praise. The stems are also incredibly sturdy, making it a great cutting variety.

As with 'Can Can', vibrant shades of all colors can be found in this mix. I source my seeds from Europe, as I have found the palette of 'Rococo' can vary greatly depending on where you buy it. Garnet red, amethyst purple, topaz, carnelian, and a fair blend of white quartz bloom freely from the seeds I grow. Although many appear to have blotches from afar, they are anything but standard or traditional. Some begin solid before spreading like rays toward the edges of the petals. Others are entirely patterned with whiskers and veining. Some have four or more colors present on a single flower, and most are richly and lavishly outlined. 'Rococo' really is a unique variety.

SPECIES
Viola ×wittrockiana

BLOOM SIZE
Medium, 1½ to 2¼ inches
(4 to 5.5 cm)

HEIGHT
10 inches (25 cm)

CUTTING STEM LENGTH
18 inches (46 cm)

FRAGRANCE
Mild

COLOR
Garnet, amethyst, topaz, white

'Spanish Eyes'

SPECIES
Viola ×wittrockiana

BLOOM SIZE
Medium, 1½ to 2½ inches
(4 to 6 cm)

HEIGHT
10 inches (25 cm)

CUTTING STEM LENGTH
18 inches (46 cm)

FRAGRANCE
None detected

COLOR
Deep violet purple, white

I believe this is the only bicolor pansy I grow. I love mixes and varying shades, but I am not normally drawn to two-tone flowers. This one is the exception.

The primary color of 'Spanish Eyes' is rich violet purple, a dark, inky shade so ardent it gives the illusion of being indefinite, as if you could slip right into the petals and disappear into a velveteen abyss. This deep pool of color streaks out in multiple small rays toward an all-encompassing perimeter of alabaster white. The eye is a vivid gold, which adds an elegant symmetry and centers the flower's voluminous petals. Many of the blooms appear as a perfect circle, in a nod to the form of the nineteenth-century show pansies.

Flowers give you exceptional freedom to experiment with colors completely outside your normal liking. In fact, they implore you to push outside your choices of habit. Every flower adds beauty, even those not in our established preferences. If you don't find a trial variety endearing, you are under no obligation to grow again. Nothing is to be lost in being bold or adventurous when it comes to growing flowers. I have been surprised by the colors and patterns I have grown fond of during my trialing of pansies and violas, and 'Spanish Eyes' is definitely one of those surprises.

'Sweet Pea Mix'

SPECIES
Viola ×wittrockiana

BLOOM SIZE
Medium, 1¼ to 2 inches
(3 to 5 cm)

HEIGHT
12 inches (30 cm)

CUTTING STEM LENGTH
20 inches (50 cm)

FRAGRANCE
Mild

COLOR
White, blush pink, lilac,
faded mauve, apricot

This was my most anticipated variety during the first season I trialed it. I came across the seeds in a catalog while I was hunting down additional sources for the beloved 'Chianti Mix' (see page 103). There was very little information, and the seeds were more expensive than any other variety I had tried, but I felt the purchase would surely be worth it.

Straight from Italy, 'Sweet Pea Mix' was a very welcome addition. I was informed by the breeder that the color can shift depending on the weather, and my first trial found a majority of the flowers blooming in white. My next trial found all the shades I had been so impatiently waiting for: orchid pink, lilac purple, antiqued gold, and faded mauve. Some had streaks and others had astonishing veining. The shape of the pansies as they open recalls the shape of a sweet pea, which may be the reason for the name. The colors in these delicate blooms are similar to 'Chianti Mix', but whereas 'Chianti Mix' flowers open in frills and flounces with reckless abandon and no regard for form or proportion, 'Sweet Pea Mix' holds a bit truer to its unique mimic of *Lathyrus odoratus*.

Waraku 'Midnight Moon'

When pansies were first hybridized, the colors that were most difficult to produce were actually true red and true blue. Bronze, copper, toffee, and mahogany brown were present in many of the older varieties. Nowadays, we have ample pansies in shades of red and blue and very few in shades of brown. This is clearly a matter of changing trends and preferences within the flower industry, and I, for one, am relieved to see more pansies available in that metallic and earthy range of colors again.

The Waraku series is a beautiful new addition to the world of pansies from Japan. They come in pink, strawberry, tangerine, apricot, white, yellow, red, and several other colors. 'Midnight Moon' is the only one I have trialed so far, but I am certainly captivated by it. The three lower petals are a melting mix of bronze, copper, and molten gold, the upper petals a gradient of bright violet to glowing lilac blue, and the deep mahogany whiskers complement the overall display. The cold hardiness of the variety allows the flowers to cheerfully smile up at you through even the chilliest months.

SPECIES
Viola ×wittrockiana

BLOOM SIZE
Medium, 1¼ to 2 inches
(3 to 5 cm)

HEIGHT
8 inches (20 cm)

CUTTING STEM LENGTH
12 inches (30 cm)

FRAGRANCE
Mild

COLOR
Sienna brown to bronze, violet to lilac blue

'Antique Laeta'

SPECIES
Viola cornuta

BLOOM SIZE
Small, ¾ to 1 inch
(2 to 2.5 cm)

HEIGHT
6 inches (15 cm)

CUTTING STEM LENGTH
Not suitable for long-stem
cutting

FRAGRANCE
None detected

COLOR
Pink, apricot, gold, cream

If you are in search of varieties perfectly suited for a pot, 'Antique Laeta' is one of my personal favorites. Considered a dwarf viola, the flowers are less than 1 inch (2.5 cm) in diameter. They bloom on small, straight, delicate stalks and rarely do they grow above a modest 6 inches (15 cm). The shape is closer to *Viola lutea*, but it brings with it the benefits of *V. cornuta*, in that it does better through frost and colder temperatures than many other varieties.

With its demure size, enchanting colors, and precocious face, this little gem is anything but ordinary. The petals look like lemon-raspberry marmalade mixed with fresh custard, and a deep, dark plum blotch gathers right around the eye. Simply put, it is very easy to fall in love with this sweet and distinctive variety.

'Arkwright Ruby'

If you have never grown pansies or violas from seed and are looking to try a variety for the purpose of cutting flowers, this is the one I most highly recommend. If I could pin a little gold star on its leaves, I would. I have grown 'Arkwright Ruby' every year since I first began my trials, and it always manages to surpass every other variety with consistency of stem length. I initially tried it in raised beds, where it confidently grew upward to between 14 and 16 inches (35.5 and 40 cm). It self-seeded the following season and took its place among my roses where, with further support from their canopy of branches, it averaged 22 inches (56 cm) in height. More recently, I have been growing 'Arkwright Ruby' at the base of my sweet peas, where it has responded to their influence, reaching 36 inches (91 cm) by the end of summer.

Deep garnet, mulled wine, ruby with a translucent cast of copper, and winter's crimson fill the petals, while the honey-golden eye rests fully encased in a concentrated mahogany blotch. As the flower ages, it can shift ever so slightly, with puddles of terra-cotta spreading gently toward the edges.

The shades of red 'Arkwright Ruby' displays are so rich and ardent that they can prove the exception even for those who may abhor red flowers. Plus, this valorous variety blooms relentlessly throughout the season. It's a true champion in my garden.

SPECIES
Viola cornuta

BLOOM SIZE
Medium, 1 to 2 inches
(2.5 to 5 cm)

HEIGHT
12 inches (30 cm)

CUTTING STEM LENGTH
24 inches (61 cm)

FRAGRANCE
Moderate

COLOR
Garnet, crimson, scarlet red

'Brush Strokes'

SPECIES
Viola cornuta

BLOOM SIZE
Small, 1¼ to 1½ inches
(3 to 4 cm)

HEIGHT
8 inches (20 cm)

CUTTING STEM LENGTH
18 inches (46 cm)

FRAGRANCE
Moderate

COLOR
Mauve, eggplant, rose,
gold, cream

Looking as though they were plucked from a Renoir canvas, shades of plum, puce, mauve, topaz, lilac, and even blush appear to be brushed across the petals of this magnificent viola. Invoking images of a streaked sky at dawn, no other variety has such splendid variation, as each and every flower is unique. While some flowers may bloom solid in color, most will be splashed or striped with an array of varying shades. The extraordinary variety that appears from bloom to bloom makes this one of the most well-regarded pansies available today.

Whenever I share photos of this variety, inquiries follow. Rarely have people seen a flower so unique. Luckily, because of an increase in both the attention and praise it deserves, it is becoming increasingly more available. As this variety ages, the color fades slightly, taking on a hint of blue that makes it a perfect focal point or accompaniment in an old rose or English-style garden. Its exceptional color and patterns also make this variety a wonderful addition to bouquet work. I find it a striking component in late-summer bouquets with other annuals rich in burgundies and golds. It has a lovely scent, and stems can reach 18 inches (46 cm) when grown for cutting.

Caramel 'Angelo'

The Caramel series has several shades that are worth growing. I sourced my seeds for these varieties from Italy and found the quality to be exceptional. My most recent trials included 'Angelo', 'Bronze Lilac', 'Pastel Lilac', and 'Blue Liberty'.

'Angelo' is one of the more delicately shaded varieties of violas that I grow. Tiny, dark purple whiskers on a light yellow flush of color contributes to the sweetest face over the cream petals. The flowers are further accentuated with splashes of the palest blue occasionally fading to barely gray. Varying temperatures will bring in shades of lavender or pink, and the color always looks as though it was brushed on by a watercolorist. The bloom is worth a lingering gaze to take in the remarkable detail of the color gently washing over the petals.

SPECIES
Viola hybrida

BLOOM SIZE
Small, 1¼ to 1½ inches (3 to 4 cm)

HEIGHT
10 inches (25 cm)

CUTTING STEM LENGTH
14 inches (35.5 cm)

FRAGRANCE
None detected

COLOR
Creamy white with yellow, splashes of pale blue, occasional lavender and pink

Deltini 'Copperfield'

The violas I love most are the intoxicatingly fragrant profuse bloomers, and this is one of them. Although the larger faces of pansies make them an ideal focal flower in gardens and bouquets, sometimes you want a flower that's a bit more delicate. 'Copperfield' is an excellent choice for adding tiny touches of copper.

If you enjoy the shades of 'Honeybee' (see page 173), you will love 'Copperfield'. When it first opens, its face is a gentle pale yellow. Rich mahogany saturates the upper petals and frames the lower petals, giving the impression the little viola is blushing. In time, the mahogany fades first to a gleaming copper, before settling into a warm gold ever so lightly touched by bronze. The yellow and mahogany of the lower petal eventually bleed together into a rich honey chestnut. This is when I think it is at its most lovely, when all the colors have blended together to make a little swirling pool of luminescence. It has a delicate auburn blotch at its center and cinnamon whiskers, giving an expression of warmth and contentment.

SPECIES
Viola cornuta

BLOOM SIZE
Small, 1¼ to 1½ inches
(3 to 4 cm)

HEIGHT
10 inches (25 cm)

CUTTING STEM LENGTH
20 inches (50 cm)

FRAGRANCE
Strong

COLOR
Golden to honey yellow, copper, mahogany

Gem 'Apricot Antique'

SPECIES
Viola hybrida

BLOOM SIZE
Small, 1¼ to 1½ inches
(3 to 4 cm)

HEIGHT
10 inches (25 cm)

CUTTING STEM LENGTH
18 inches (46 cm)

FRAGRANCE
Strong

COLOR
Caramel, toffee, honey,
raspberry, mauve

Gem 'Apricot Antique' is the smallest member of the "antique trifecta," as I lovingly refer to them. Imperial 'Antique Shades' (see page 125), Nature 'Antique Shades' (see page 134), and Gem 'Apricot Antique' are all poured from the same palette and all beautifully complement one another. While the bloom size is a bit smaller, the stem length is still equivalent to its larger flowered friends. Unique to 'Apricot Antique', though, is the opaline violet veining that flows throughout the upper petals. While it displays similar shades of caramel, toffee, honey, raspberry, and mauve, this opalescent cast gives it a mystic shimmer like summer clouds at dusk during the early moments of a lightning storm. If you need a little wisp of magic in your floral work, this variety may be it.

The Gem series is exceptional in that it has a much higher heat tolerance than many violas while still being able to withstand the frosty temperatures of late fall and early spring. It also blooms earlier than most violas. All of this has earned it awards with Netherlands-based Fleuroselect, an international organization for the ornamental plant industry.

'Hobbit Mungo'

I don't grow many white pansies or violas. It is not that they have any mentionable faults. It is a matter of preference. While 'Hobbit Mungo' is not entirely white, its full, rounded shape and white upper petals make it look mostly white from afar. As such, it is my favorite white viola to grow.

Admittedly, the reason I added this variety to my trials in the first place was not appearance but name. Although as soon as it bloomed, I was totally smitten. I have found it has a good fragrance, making it great for pots, but I also tend to plant it at the base of my softer yellow roses. It is not a variety I recommend for cutting, but if you are looking for a white or light yellow viola for your garden, this one is as sweet as they come.

SPECIES
Viola cornuta

BLOOM SIZE
Small, 1 to 1½ inches
(2.5 to 4 cm)

HEIGHT
8 inches (20 cm)

CUTTING STEM LENGTH
Not suitable for long-stem cutting

FRAGRANCE
Moderate

COLOR
Lemon to honey yellow, milky white

'Irish Molly'

SPECIES
Viola hybrida

BLOOM SIZE
Medium, 1¼ to 2 inches
(3 to 5 cm)

HEIGHT
8 inches (20 cm)

CUTTING STEM LENGTH
Not suitable for long-stem
cutting

FRAGRANCE
Moderate

COLOR
Topaz, bronze, chocolate,
olive

Similar in uniqueness to 'Envy' (see page 108), 'Irish Molly' holds inimitable hues among her petals. Antiqued gold ebbs beneath a small umber pool surrounding the eye and spreading in shadowed rays across the lower petals. As the luminous yellow shifts to topaz and bronze, it further clouds over with an opaque chocolate veil covering the entirety of the upper petals. The whole flower seems to take on an olive undernote, and at times you can see a faint hint of smalt blue.

This is one of the older varieties still available today. I could not confidently trace its exact origin, but I was able to find mention of it shortly after World War II. Roy Genders refers to his 'Irish Molly' plants as having thrived for over a decade, being healthy, free flowering, and "well-nigh indestructible." This is the only variety of viola and pansy that I do not grow from seed. I ordered in a handful of plants some years back, and they have, just as Mr. Genders attested, come back year after year with no additional fuss or protection from our zone 8a winters. I have not found it well suited for cutting, but it is an exceptional choice in the garden. It does require frequent and diligent deadheading to keep it healthy and in flush.

'Miniola Heart Aqua'

Violas in the shape of a heart that boast pale aqua-blue petals—how can you possibly resist giving such a variety a try? This incredibly cold-tolerant viola blooms in as little as six weeks, which is half the time of most violas and pansies.

With shades of lemon to mustard yellow beneath dark contrasting whiskers, its dainty face appears to be suppressing an innocent little chortle. The petals gently fade toward the edges with shades of smoky lavender, foggy gray, and the palest of aqua blue. This is a wonderful variety for adding a spot of luminescence without being overly bright or bold.

SPECIES
Viola hybrida

BLOOM SIZE
Small, 1 to 1¼ inches
(2.5 to 3 cm)

HEIGHT
8 inches (20 cm)

CUTTING STEM LENGTH
12 inches (30 cm)

FRAGRANCE
Moderate

COLOR
Golden to mustard yellow, aqua blue to light gray

Sorbet 'Antique Shades'

SPECIES
Viola cornuta

BLOOM SIZE
Small, 1 to 1¼ inches
(2.5 to 3 cm)

HEIGHT
8 inches (20 cm)

CUTTING STEM LENGTH
12 inches (30 cm)

FRAGRANCE
Mild

COLOR
Purple, burgundy, claret,
gold, white

The Sorbet series of violas has an abundance of color options, and I grow many of them every season. They are both heat and cold tolerant, so their bloom window is very long, and they can be grown in almost all zones. They also seem to attract the bees just a bit more than other varieties, making them an excellent choice for pollinator gardens. The Sorbet series is readily available in nurseries and through seed.

This particular variety looks as though each and every flower was painted by hand. No two are exactly alike. The primary color can range from claret to garnet or from plum to amethyst. The eye always remains a bright gold, but varied shades of white, cream, or yellow will be found gently encompassing it. The rays are a deep eggplant, and although they stay close near the top of the eye, they flow into vivid veining across the entire lower petal. The colors of the lower petal are a blend of all the shades in which this viola can be found, as if the artist felt compelled to use every last bit of paint, so none would go to waste. Quite the little masterpiece, this one.

Sorbet 'Honeybee'

In trying to narrow down my favorites of all the colors available in the Sorbet series, 'Honeybee' is my first pick. Some flowers have modest blotches and others just a few whiskers, but all of them have faces drawn in fresh espresso. It is impossible to count how many shades of yellow and brown are found among blooms—from honey to caramel, toffee to pecan, cinnamon to sienna. The veining varies from milk to dark chocolate, spilling over at times and filling the petals with the color of rich brown syrup. If you love the deep golden shades of late summer and early fall, 'Honeybee' is the best of them.

I find golden violas to be wonderfully exuberant. It is as if the sun rained down tiny droplets in winter to provide good cheer and hope, and those little beads of liquid light and warmth bloomed into tiny golden violas.

SPECIES
Viola cornuta

BLOOM SIZE
Small, 1 to 1½ inches
(2.5 to 4 cm)

HEIGHT
8 inches (20 cm)

CUTTING STEM LENGTH
12 inches (30 cm)

FRAGRANCE
Mild

COLOR
Gold, honey, caramel, toffee, cinnamon, chocolate

Sorbet 'Orchid Rose Beacon'

SPECIES
Viola cornuta

BLOOM SIZE
Small, 1 to 1¼ inches
(2.5 to 3 cm)

HEIGHT
8 inches (20 cm)

CUTTING STEM LENGTH
12 inches (30 cm)

FRAGRANCE
Mild

COLOR
White, violet, amethyst,
orchid, magenta

The combination of colors on 'Orchid Rose Beacon' is pure enchantment. The upper petals are of the purest white, while the lower three petals hold a lagoon of changing hues. From the outer edges, faint amethyst veining creates an opalescent web that increases in vividity as it reaches toward the golden eye. At its depth, the violet pool appears charged with an electric current that gives fleeting glimpses of a lapis-blue glow. Toward the shallows, it lightens to magenta and then orchid before washing away entirely back to white.

There are several pansies with the 'Beacon Rose' coloring, but I don't think any of them are as bewitching as this one. Although the Sorbet series has a smaller bloom size, it is not any less desirable. In fact, its availability gives it additional merit.

Sorbet 'Phantom'

From the original *Viola tricolor* that played a role in the origination of the garden pansy to the wild violas that still grow in Europe, pansies and violas will always be associated with the color purple. In the countless conversations I have enjoyed about these flowers, there is always someone who prefers them in purple over every other color. I think you can argue that pansies and violas boast more magnificent shades of purple than any other flower, and Sorbet 'Phantom' is one of them.

While the soft white face varies in size from barely encircling the eye to encompassing the majority of the three lower petals, the outer portion of the petals is consistently of the deepest blackened plum. Some flowers exhibit an abundant pool of gold, and others reveal only a touch right at the eye. These blooms remind me of toast with butter and plum jam. They are truly delectable and a favorite of mine for use in baking.

SPECIES
Viola cornuta

BLOOM SIZE
Small, 1 to 1¼ inches
(2.5 to 3 cm)

HEIGHT
8 inches (20 cm)

CUTTING STEM LENGTH
16 inches (40 cm)

FRAGRANCE
Mild

COLOR
White, violet, amethyst, orchid, magenta

Sorbet 'XP Neptune'

SPECIES
Viola cornuta

BLOOM SIZE
Small, 1 to 1¼ inches
(2.5 to 3 cm)

HEIGHT
8 inches (20 cm)

CUTTING STEM LENGTH
12 inches (30 cm)

FRAGRANCE
Mild

COLOR
White, ultraviolet, indigo,
ink, plum

Whenever I see this viola, I think of the ocean and Neptune, the mythological god of the sea. Hurricane-force winds, dark, murky waters, and beckoning Sirens often swirl in my thoughts. Look close enough at it petals and you can almost feel the breath of the kraken on the back of your neck. The outer edges on some, as with the heart of the sea, are so darkly soaked in indigo they appear close to black. As you drift toward the eye of the bloom, the watery shades soften to sapphire and cobalt before diluting completely to white. It is because of this contrast that you can truly see the depth of color, unlike other varieties that are wholly blue. The intense inky whiskers add further allure to this aquatic beauty.

I have also considered, what if the inspiration for this smalt-blue gem was actually in the stars and not the seas? The planet Neptune is frigid, blustery, and dark. When shown on maps and in pictures, it is almost always in hues of blue. The palette of Neptune that so aptly links to the ocean displays the same ultraviolet and deep indigo shades characteristic of the night sky.

Whichever you prefer, sea or stars, I recommend giving this variety a try.

Sorbet 'XP Pink Halo'

If you enjoy the smaller size of violas but still desire unique hues and characteristics, this variety is sure to please you. To quote Shakespeare's *A Midsummer Night's Dream,* "Though she be but little she is fierce." Violas are well known for having expressions on their little faces, and this one is especially telling.

This aptly named flower boasts a beaming halo framing the eye and deep plum whiskers. The halo can vary from mauve to magenta pink, or fuchsia to orchid purple. Because the outer portion of the petals is always a pristine white, the flower looks as though she dipped her eager face in a fresh blackberry pie. There's a bit of mischief to this one.

SPECIES
Viola cornuta

BLOOM SIZE
Small, 1 to 1¼ inches
(2.5 to 3 cm)

HEIGHT
8 inches (20 cm)

CUTTING STEM LENGTH
12 inches (30 cm)

FRAGRANCE
Mild

COLOR
White, pink, orchid
purple

'Tiger Eye'

SPECIES
Viola cornuta

BLOOM SIZE
Small, 1 to 1¼ inches
(2.5 to 3 cm)

HEIGHT
10 inches (25 cm)

CUTTING STEM LENGTH
16 inches (40 cm)

FRAGRANCE
Strong

COLOR
Red, yellow, or mixed

Of all the violas I have grown, this is the one I have found to be the most fragrant. Walking among its blooms in the warm afternoon sun, you will be transported to the shop of the finest chocolatier. 'Tiger Eye' comes in two solid variations, yellow and red, one the color of liquid sunshine with deep chocolate-brown veining and the other the color of cinnamon with deep espresso veining. It is not uncommon to see the latter fade from warm cinnamon red to a golden honey, all within the same bloom. The contrasting dark veining across the entire flower is what separates this viola from all others.

The bloom size is petite, and long stems can be grown for cutting, which makes 'Tiger Eye' a suitable bloom for smaller bouquets and arrangements. The variety overwinters well when planted in gardens with mild climates. It is also tolerant of the heat, and if kept in good soil and deadheaded frequently, it will bloom continuously throughout the growing season, making it one of the best accompaniment flowers for pots and landscaping. If the pattern doesn't convince you to grow it in abundance, the fragrance surely will.

Black Pansies and Violas

I've always been drawn to black flowers. While they are usually the result of hybridization and careful cultivation, there is something about them that I find incredibly enchanting and grounding. Although they are commonly associated with gothic gardens or seasonal celebrations, I believe they offer much more. No flower I have ever seen has petals as truly velvety as the black pansy. They are like the cloak of night, full of tranquility, with a little golden eye twinkling back at you.

It's been argued that flowers do not bloom true black and are instead intensely dark shades of red or purple. I feel it's a question of opinion. While science can dictate a great deal, it cannot mandate how we see varied shades of color or beauty. One person's pink is another person's red. Gray often blurs into blue. If a flower appears to the eye as completely and utterly black, can we not then accept it as black? Whichever side of this debate you find yourself on, I think we can all agree that black flowers, few and far between as they are, are at the very least genuinely intriguing.

The color black has long had two completely opposite occasions and personas—be it in clothing, flowers, furniture, or décor. In one role, it is the color regularly called on to represent darkness and death. The black pansy, in particular, has been a flower representing loss. In *Flora Symbolica; or, the Language of Flowers,* written by John Ingram in 1869, pansies are said to represent thoughts, sentiment, or "think of me." In my years of study, I have come across countless lockets, brooches, and rings bearing black pansies or violas alongside a loved one's initials. What better flower to hold near and seek comfort from when missing someone once so close? The black pansy is certainly a just choice to accompany a broken heart. But that's only half of what the color can mean.

The other role black prominently fulfills just as often, if not more often, is that of elegance, simplicity, class, and good taste. Luxurious black cars. Refined black furniture. Black-tie affairs. Chic black overcoats and classic black pants that go with absolutely everything. And nothing will ever replicate the role the little black dress has played in fashion. As Coco Chanel said, "Simplicity is the keynote of all true elegance." Even renowned artist Georgia O'Keeffe found inspriation in the black pansy and portrayed it with true elegance in her painting *Black Pansy & Forget-Me-Nots (Pansy)*, painted in 1926.

Black pansies, for me, will always be the latter. There are no flowers I find more soothingly elegant than long-stemmed black pansies. They are the "little black dress" of flowers and are always the right choice.

My favorite vase featuring my favorite flower, the black pansy

'Accord Black Beauty'

SPECIES
Viola ×wittrockiana

BLOOM SIZE
Medium, 1½ to 2 inches
(4 to 5 cm)

HEIGHT
8 inches (20 cm)

CUTTING STEM LENGTH
22 inches (56 cm)

FRAGRANCE
Mild

COLOR
Black

I have been growing this variety for several years, and I think it to be one of the most beautifully shaped of all the black pansies available. Its petals bear a much greater resemblance to *Viola grandiflora* or *V. tricolor* than the modern garden pansy. Gentle veining on the rich ebony petals almost make it shimmer, and some blooms hint to the slightest bit of ruffling as you near the edges. I have found the first flush of flowers to be the most intense, and they tend to shift to a very dark, inky purple as the temperatures warm later in the summer.

Black pansies are exceptional when creating an impact through a monotone arrangement. This variety, in particular, looks exceptional with the black varieties of bearded irises, as most black irises have the same deep, inky purple sheen just below the surface. Paired with a smooth matte black vase, they are politely decorous and fashionably understated, befitting any grand affair.

'Atlas Black'

'Atlas' tends to bloom closer in shape to the original garden pansy. It has large, velvety petals with a gentle fluttered texture, and the edges vary from smooth to fully scalloped. It is a very deep, rich black, like soot, and it does exceptionally well in winter.

High anthocyanin (antioxidant) content is responsible for colors like red, blue, purple, and black in flowers. Although it is believed pollinators are not as attracted to dark flowers in general, black does give the flower a higher internal temperature, which potentially attracts the pollinators by alternative means. From the humble speculation of an observant grower, I always see just as many bees and butterflies on my black pansies as I do on every other shade.

SPECIES
Viola ×wittrockiana

BLOOM SIZE
Large, 2 to 2½ inches
(5 to 6 cm)

HEIGHT
8 inches (20 cm)

CUTTING STEM LENGTH
18 inches (46 cm)

FRAGRANCE
None detected

COLOR
Black

'Black Devil'

SPECIES
Viola ×wittrockianaa

BLOOM SIZE
Large, 1¾ to 3 inches
(4.5 to 7.5 cm)

HEIGHT
8 inches (20 cm)

CUTTING STEM LENGTH
20 inches (50 cm)

FRAGRANCE
None detected

COLOR
Black

Larger in size, with blooms up to 3 inches (7.5 cm), 'Black Devil' seems to have the most inconsistencies of all the black varieties I grow. This is not necessarily a mark against it, as I rather enjoy seeing so much variation from flower to flower. The color is reliably dark, like pitch, and the only time I usually see a hint of purple is after a good downpour when deep amethyst droplets drip from the petals.

The shape and size are where the variance comes into play. It's unruly. Contrary. Mischievous even. Some blooms barely reach 2 inches (5 cm), while others are almost double that. The petals may be rounded and uniform, or they may be furrowed and rumpled like the blankets of a child's bed after a late-morning nap. Sometimes the top petals are larger and sometimes they are smaller. The edges may be scalloped or smooth. It seems as though it is intent on defying expectations. The only thing you can reasonably assume is that every flower will be, without doubt, astonishingly beautiful.

'Black King'

If you are going to grow only one variety of black pansy, this is one to consider. Unlike most pansies and violas that have a delectable scent invoking almonds, honey, or chocolate, 'Black King' has a lighter fragrance that hints to *Viola odorata,* which is a bit sweeter and traditionally floral. All black pansies appear velvety, but this one, in particular, looks to be made of thick, plush velour. The shade of black has an iridescent violet undertone like you can sometimes see on the feathers of a raven when the sunlight hits them just right. In contrast, some blooms will appear entirely deep purple with an opaque onyx shadow about them. The petals are less scalloped than other varieties, with the bloom's presentation more uniformly rounded and neat.

This is a great variety for culinary work. I've seen it incorporated into syrups and jams, adorning waffles and cakes, baked into muffins, and stirred into yogurts. I make my boys pumpkin spice muffins with cream cheese frosting in the fall, and these pansies are an exemplary topping.

SPECIES
Viola xwittrockiana

BLOOM SIZE
Large, 2 to 3 inches
(5 to 7.5 cm)

HEIGHT
8 inches (20 cm)

CUTTING STEM LENGTH
16 inches (40 cm)

FRAGRANCE
Mild

COLOR
Purple to black

'Black Prince'

SPECIES
Viola ×wittrockiana

BLOOM SIZE
Medium, 1¼ to 2 inches
(3 to 5 cm)

HEIGHT
10 inches (25 cm)

CUTTING STEM LENGTH
22 inches (56 cm)

FRAGRANCE
None detected

COLOR
Black

One of the first varieties to germinate each year when I sow my pansy and viola seeds, 'Black Prince' has always proven reliable and steadfast in my garden. It has a shape that might best be described as romantic. Full and curved, its gracefully proportioned petals almost form a heart rather than a circle. Its flowers are not overly large, but when gathered together and filling a vase, they are absolutely striking. Of all the black varieties I have grown, this one is my favorite.

'Black Prince' is also one of the best varieties for cut-flower work. In early spring, I love to arrange a dozen or two alongside peonies of creamy vanilla and cherry blossom pink. As summer draws near, they are a sophisticated companion to apricot roses and smoky-gray larkspur. Nearing early fall, I often pair them with blush, ivory, and black dahlias. Just as black goes with any color given that the presentation is in good taste, I have found the same to be true with these pansies.

Flamenco 'Black Moon'

As with its Flamenco series kin, 'Terracotta' and 'Tricolor Rose' (see pages 113 and 114, respectively), you can expect beautiful ruffling and crinkled edges all around 'Black Moon'. The color is a rich coal black, and the flowers are full and well formed. This is the newest addition to the black varieties I have grown, and I've had great success with germination thus far.

This variety seems to be more readily available now both by seed and through mail-order starts, likely because it is considered one of the most splendid black flowers currently in cultivation. The Flamenco series is an amazing group, and this is another must-try color within it.

SPECIES
Viola ×wittrockiana

BLOOM SIZE
Medium, 1½ to 2½ inches (4 to 6 cm)

HEIGHT
10 inches (25 cm)

CUTTING STEM LENGTH
18 inches (46 cm)

FRAGRANCE
Mild

COLOR
Black

CHAPTER 4

Seasonal Arrangements with Pansies and Violas

There is a special kind of magic in using seasonal flowers in arrangements. First, you must open your mind to what Mother Nature is offering you. Let her lift the veil away from all the flowers, branches, and foliage you had previously failed to see. Using seasonal flowers also forces you to stretch the bounds of your imagination. Removing the popular flowers we often default to from our floral cache makes us look to alternatives that we may have never before considered. Many seasonal flowers are adversely affected by transport yet well suited for floral design. These are best grown in your own garden or sourced locally. While they may not be not as popular as the rose, carnation, and lily, they can be just astounding in color, form, and presence. You may even find that these alternatives, like the viola and pansy, become your new favorites.

I have always seen the seasonal shift of flowers like a marvelous performance in two acts. It starts with an overture of the hellebores. The curtain opens, and with it, the darkness of winter gently evaporates. The hellebores are already in midturn, putting on a lovely display of their final blooms before they exit the stage, leaving a brief moment of stillness.

Then we begin the first act, spring. The opening scene sees the anemones and daffodils emerging from the thawing soil. Frost covers them in a morning robe of glimmer and shine, but by the third scene, the snow has ceased, and the stage brightens under the warmth of the afternoon sun. The tulips make their entrance in the fourth scene, swaying back and forth across the stage with the exuberance of April's winds. The fifth and sixth scenes see the ranunculus intertwining with the tulips and daffodils, creating a sea of color and texture in vibrant oranges, lemon yellows, and salmon pinks. The next scene, with the fringes and frills of the tulips and countless satin ruffles of ranunculus, sees the entire stage saturated in radiant spinning tutus, while the intoxicating

A midsummer wedding bouquet featuring over two dozen long-stemmed pansies and violas

fragrance of the daffodils and hyacinths swirls about. The rose makes her first appearance at this time, a refined ebb and flow in and out of the spotlight. The final scene of spring slows to a quiet lull, as amethyst and ivory lilacs gently usher out the season's vivid hues.

It is now intermission, the pause between the first act of spring and the second act of summer. This is the pas de deux between the peony and the bearded iris. Dreamlike and fully elegant, it begins with slow graceful movements in lilac, blush, and pearl before shifting to bold spins and astonishing leaps in crimson red, Byzantium purple, and black. They hold the spotlight through the month of May, providing incredible beauty while we transition out of spring, and are the signal that summer is about to begin. They warn you, with their brief intermission, that only a few days are left until you will be fully engaged and unable to pause. There are no idle moments in summer for those who grow flowers.

And so begins the second act, summer. In the first scene, perennials fill the stage with grasses and shrubs, while slender branches unfurl their emerald leaves and blossoms throughout the eaves above the stage. The rose is present, and remains so until the final curtain falls. Scenes two and three see the annuals making their way into the spotlight: sweet peas, larkspur, and stock glide in from stage left; snapdragons, nigella, and phlox from stage right; and the zinnias, poppies, and amaranth saunter right down the aisles. By scene six, they all come together, putting on a show so grand you almost feel as though you can't quite keep up. Scene seven introduces the dahlias, which do their best to steal the show and proclaim themselves the real prima ballerina. They exit in the final scene with a dramatic tantrum of brown stalks and blackened petals, having been forced offstage by the first frost and the closing of the curtain.

The chorus of pansies—which has been present in every scene from the beginning of spring through the end of summer, accompanying and matching all the other flowers in grace, beauty, and performance—remains and ends the show on the loveliest note possible. Even as we begin to leave, the second act of summer having ended and the curtain closed, the pansies linger, waving goodbye with their expressive faces winking and twinkling. A standing ovation, a whirlwind performance—how did it pass so quickly? The pansies leave us filled with hope and a renewed sense of tenacity, and we find ourselves already looking forward to next year's show.

My awe of this seasonal shift and my love for arranging bouquets stretch back to childhood. As a young child, I remember taking flowers from neighboring fields and creating small bouquets. As a teenager, I found myself disappointed with the arrangements available in local florist shops. They seemed so unnatural. The flowers, so perfectly formed and entirely identical to one another, barely seemed real. The roses had no fragrance. There was no wonder within the petals and no magic within the leaves. In my early twenties, I would buy several small bundles of flowers from the local grocer (all that was available to me at the time) and create my own arrangements at home. Some I would keep, but many I would give to friends and family. I did not have a large garden to pick from regularly, and I wasn't even aware of the idea of a cutting garden or a flower farm for many more years. I worked with what I could find and made the arrangements as beautiful as possible, placing each flower in a way that allowed it to be seen.

A couple of decades later, I have found myself growing all the flowers I love most—including pansies and violas—and making them into the arrangements I think they deserve. For me, arranging flowers is like painting. My bouquets are full of intention, and I pour a great deal of emotion into them. I select every stem as an individual before bringing all my choices together as a whole. Each one is placed in a way that supports the beauty of the bouquet while ensuring its individuality remains discernible. I hope my approach translates for others. I am not professionally trained in making bouquets, but I have been fortunate to study a bit here and there with some incredibly talented professionals, and I have taken several excellent courses over the years. My bouquets are a reflection of how I think the flowers deserve to be seen.

Whether using seasonal local flowers, flowers that are easily and financially accessible, or flowers that were ordered with meticulous forethought and planning, one of the best things about making carefully crafted bouquets and arrangements is that each one is sure to be as unique as the individual making it. You can give a dozen florists the same flowers, and chances are, every bouquet will look different. You don't have to be professionally trained or qualified to make bouquets and arrangements for your home. There is no rule book. Fill your home with flowers. Create vases of joy and wonder and have fun while doing it. My own arrangements are meant not as a how-to but as inspiration. Encouragement. A little nudge forward. Fill a vase, a bowl, or a jar. The vessel does not have to be intricate or expensive. If you find it beautiful, then beautiful it is. Pansies, especially, have the ability to bring elegance and beauty into your home just as they do in the garden, and they should be given the chance to do so at every available opportunity.

LATE SPRING

Late spring brings some of the most beautiful flowers for arranging into bloom all at once. For this arrangement, I chose to use hues that evoke the freshness of spring. It is the time of year for witnessing the faded shades of winter dissolve back beneath the freshly thawed earth, for feeling a cool breeze flit through your hair while the sun warms your cheeks, for watching umber bark become steadily covered by the unfurling of leaves.

All four focal flowers—peony, bearded iris, rose, pansy—in this arrangement bloom in a broad range of colors, but the pansy and bearded iris, in particular, bloom in almost every shade imaginable of red, orange, yellow, blue, purple, and black.

I prefer garden roses over other roses for spring, as they are so soft and inviting and their fragrance never disappoints. The irises and pansies are also fragrant, making these flowers just as lovely to smell as they are to look at.

PEONY: 'Early Glow'
BEARDED IRISES: 'Rite of Passage', 'Haunted Heart'
ROSES: 'Ash Wednesday', 'Léontine Gervais', 'Crocus Rose', 'Colette'
PANSIES: Delta 'Pink Shades', Flamenco 'Terracotta', Inspire 'Peach Shades', 'Moulin Rouge', along with some additional violas that self-seeded throughout the garden

BLACK IRISES AND PANSIES

Black pansies and irises are a favorite of mine. Their velvety petals display such profound depth. They are so rich and so elegant, luxurious even.

As noted earlier, I know that black flowers are not to everyone's liking. The same can be said for red flowers, orange flowers, and yellow flowers. It is all a matter of preference. Our preferred color palette often changes throughout our lifetime, for some more than for others. I have always liked black flowers, and I am confident I always will—particularly the black pansy.

While I usually place black pansies among other shades and types of flowers, there is an attractive simplicity found in a monotone arrangement. I almost always pair black pansies with a classic white vase, but on occasion, I will select a black vase for an elevated and distinguished aesthetic.

This pairing of pansies and bearded irises has great longevity, as the spent irises can be snapped off, allowing the additional buds present on the stem to continue to open and bloom. The same is true for the pansies.

BEARDED IRISES: 'Black Mirror', 'Black Suited', 'Black Lipstick', 'Hello Darkness'
PANSIES: 'Accord Black Beauty', 'Black Prince', 'Black Devil', 'Black King'

SOFT SUMMER PINKS

Summer is full of possibilities when it comes to flowers, as all the annuals have finally burst into bloom. I gathered what caught my eye in soft shades of peach, apricot, blush, cream, and lilac for this arrangement.

Using a tall, slender vase makes arranging easy, as the height and form of the flowers themselves create the shape and dimension in the bouquet.

This bouquet is wild and free, wispy and delicate. What I love most is that it looks like it was gathered from an enchanted garden, and the fragrance is equally beguiling.

Yarrow and Queen Anne's lace are great accompaniments in summer bouquets, and I use them often. Tall, slim larkspur and stock add height. Annual phlox is my favorite filler flower, and sweet peas add further charm, plus both are wonderfully fragrant. For the sweet peas, I like using the primary stems, which include multiple flowers and tendrils. Love-in-a-mist, pincushion flower, strawflower, sweet sultan, and zinnia contribute additional color and texture.

ROSES: 'Koko Loko', 'Above and Beyond', 'Ghislaine de Féligonde'
PANSIES: 'Chianti Mix', Imperial 'Antique Shades', Inspire 'Peach Shades'

MIDSUMMER REDS

I like gathering ivory, deep red, and vivid purple flowers together. They feel deeply dramatic as a whole. Midsummer is when stems on pansies and violas get long enough for the flowers to contribute substantial height to arrangements or be used as focal flowers on their own.

'Arkwright Ruby' is one of the best violas for arrangements and bouquet work. It has some of the longest and sturdiest stems of all the varieties I have grown.

Accompanying the roses, dahlias, and pansies in this arrangement are some of my favorite summer annuals. Larkspur adds height in slender, spiky form, while chocolate lace flower and yarrow contribute circular blooms of substantial size. Amaranth provides a lovely draping effect, and annual phlox brings the color palette together in her many blooms. The deep red of the pincushion flowers, strawflowers, and sweet peas adds further depth. For extra foliage, I used raspberry greens along with eryngium, starflower, and poppy pods for a touch of uniqueness.

An antiqued gold compote suited this varied selection, and all the flowers are held in place with a large flower frog. This arrangement bloomed beautifully for well over a week, and I enjoyed every moment of it.

ROSES: 'Hot Cocoa', 'Lion's Fairy Tale'
DAHLIAS: 'Fidalgo Knight', 'Fitzy's Dark Angel', 'Tam Tam'
PANSIES AND VIOLAS: Nature 'Antique Shades', Nature 'Mulberry Shades', 'Arkwright Ruby', 'Black Prince', and a few self-sown lovelies

LATE-SUMMER BLUSH AND BLACK

Another palette that captivates me is cream, blush, and black. It is the epitome of romance.

The black pansies elevate these well-loved softer shades from ordinary and predictable to exceptional and surprising. They bring a mysterious richness, as if there is a passionate secret tucked beneath the petals. They feel almost sybaritic.

As some of the cooler annuals have ceased blooming by late summer, this bouquet is heavy in focal flowers and lighter in fillers. Accompanying the roses, dahlias, and pansies are the last few stems of larkspur, a light handful of yarrow, an immodest amount of phlox, and a touch of amaranth, eryngium, ninebark, and raspberry vines.

I enjoy including berries in bouquets when they appropriately complement the palette and occasion, as they give the overtone of a living renaissance painting.

ROSES: 'Koko Loko', 'Lion's Fairy Tale', 'Julia's Rose'
DAHLIAS: 'Café au Lait', 'Cupcake', 'Diana's Memory', 'Irish D Porter', 'Koko Puff'
PANSIES: 'Accord Black Beauty', 'Black King', 'Black Prince'

EARLY FALL

Many of my bouquets and arrangements start with one flower—one particular bloom that catches my eye above all the others. In this arrangement, it was the iris.

Almost all my irises come and go in the month of May. This one is the exception. It is a late-summer bloomer, and it surprised me when I saw it opening among the faded green leaves of the other irises as we pushed into early autumn. It has antiqued-gold standards, russet falls that shimmer through copper highlights, and a small pool of electric violet beneath the fiery orange beard. It was the ideal flower to create an arrangement around, and I had plenty of pansies blooming in complementary shades to accompany it.

I warmly embrace all that fall encompasses, as it has always been my favorite season. While it can prove a difficult time for sourcing seasonal flowers, there are always some that persist in the early warmer weeks. The dahlias, phlox, and strawflowers can usually survive a slight chill in the night air, and some roses will continue after the temperatures begin to dip. I even had a few zinnias still in bloom that I was able to tuck into this arrangement, along with some pepper berry branches, amaranth, and ninebark.

BEARDED IRIS: 'As Beauty Does'
ROSES: 'Golden Celebration', 'Pumpkin Patch', 'Butterscotch', 'Honey Dijon'
DAHLIAS: 'Bloomquist York', 'KA's Mocha Katie', 'Copper Boy', 'Crossfield Ebony', 'Koko Puff'
PANSIES: Nature 'Antique Shades', Nature 'Mulberry Shades', 'Chianti Mix', Majestic Giants 'Sherry'

END-OF-SEASON BOUQUET

Once fall sets in fully, it is time to put the garden to bed. The irises and peonies get cut back, the roses are mulched, and the dahlias are dug. The bulbs are planted and everything is tidied up for a long winter's rest—everything, that is, except the pansies. It isn't until winter really settles in that I give my pansies protection for the next few months of ice and snow, as many continue to bloom throughout the fall.

Around the time I get ready to clear the beds, I always have an occasion or two pop up where flowers are necessary. This is when I find myself really digging into unconventional sources of flowers and foliage.

As these are the last dahlias of the season, the petals have a few spots. The black-eyed Susan shows a bit of fading at her tips. The strawflower is fully open, and the leaves of the ninebark have begun to age and crispen. Grasses and rosehips are available to provide lovely fall texture, but the hydrangea leaves are tinged with scarlet and auburn. Even the pansies have a few nibbles, as the slugs have returned in force with the autumn rain. The last of the sweet pea vines are tucked in, along with a few other bits and bobs.

Do age and blemishing mean a flower is incapable of accomplishing its purpose? I don't believe so. These flowers are true to the season in which they were cut. Flowers, when brought indoors, are meant to brighten a room by adding warmth, beauty, and fragrance. They aren't meant to be the focal point. People are the focal point. A few spots and nibbles should not detract from the occasion on which they were gathered in celebration.

Many flowers are at their most beautiful just before the petals drop—when they have been well loved by the bees and butterflies, and after they have been touched by the cool night breeze and the morning dew. While this bouquet will not last for long, it is perfectly capable of warming a room for the afternoon, enhancing a dinner for an evening, or even complementing a bride who is open to carrying a handful of nature just as it is during a small seasonal ceremony.

Do not discount your flowers' worth because they are nearing the end of the season. I say, gather and celebrate them down to the last petal.

CHAPTER 5

Out of the Garden and into the Home

The Palatable Pansy

I honestly cannot think of any flower as multifaceted as the pansy and viola. While there are quite a few edible flowers, not many bloom from spring through fall, are as easy to grow, or are as lovely in bouquets. Their potential extends even further when you take them into your home. They are, in my opinion, the most beautiful of all edible flowers, and because they come in such an expansive range of colors, patterns, and sizes, there will always be plenty of options that perfectly match the food with which they are paired.

Pansies and violas are making appearances in more and more restaurants, from farm-to-table hot spots that incorporate seasonal fresh foods to Michelin star restaurants. They are effective both as a whole flower and as individual petals, adding color and texture to just about any kind of dish.

Pansy leaves are a substantial source of unconventional edible beauty as well and, like the flowers, come in several shapes and sizes. I use both the leaves and flowers in my salads year-round. One of my go-to summertime salads is spinach and strawberries, and the surprising color pansies bring to the fresh greens and juicy red berries makes the salad particularly irresistible. The ruffled varieties look especially beautiful in fall harvest salads, as their bright colors, streaks, stripes, and penciling are a good contrast with the rich, leafy greens, vegetables, and seeds.

When it comes to soup, there is nothing better on a chilly fall day than a creamy puree of delicata squash. It is the color of harvest gold, making 'Tiger Eye' violas the perfect garnish. Another soup I make often is chicken, rice, and spinach, which I load

Pansy Nature 'Antique Shades' atop an Earl Grey tea–infused cake with vanilla buttercream and white chocolate drizzle up with ginger and garlic. The recipe is from one of my favorite cookbooks, and it gives my immune system a huge boost with every bowl. In it and in other vegetable-heavy soups, I opt for deep purple pansies, as I have found warmer orange and red shades get lost among the carrots and tomatoes.

As an Italian mother to three boys, I make pasta often. Some of my recipes were passed down from my great-grandmothers, one from Sicily and the other from northern Italy. Others I have discovered, modified, and perfected over the last couple of decades on my own. Whether I'm making lasagna, gnocchi, or a simple bowl of rigatoni with sauce, you can be sure I'm going to bring in some pansies from the garden to add before serving.

As for dessert, there are several well-regarded cookbooks that incorporate edible flowers in baking. Fresh or pressed, pansies are the loveliest form of decoration. I've even seen recipes that use them in the dough of tamales, flaky pastries, and breads. If you feel a bit intimidated by advanced baking, decorating cakes and cookies is a great place to start. Pansies are an exceptional decoration for cakes, used either as they are or candied (brushed with simple syrup, allowed to dry a bit, tossed with sugar, and then allowed to dry completely). They are also an easy option for adding color and charm to cookies, whether they sit atop iced sugar cookies, delicate shortbread, or masterfully made macarons.

Pansies and violas are also wonderful floating atop bubbly Champagne or sparkling water, pressed and sugared and added to cocktails, or frozen in ice cubes for lemonade and sangria. The pansy is so versatile in the world of culinary arts that it comes as no surprise that it is now being grown alongside the herbs chefs reach for in restaurant kitchens around the world.

Top left: Squash soup with viola 'Tiger Eye'
Top right: A garden salad featuring pansy 'Frizzle Sizzle Orange'
Bottom left: Pansy Inspire 'Peach Shades' floating atop a frothy cocktail
Bottom right: Pressed pansies adorn the tops of macarons

SYR. VIOLÆ

Flores
Viola Tricol:

CULPEPER'S COMPLETE HERBAL

Apothecary and Health

Pansies and violas have a long history in apothecary and were used to treat multiple ailments for centuries. In fact, it wasn't until 1926 that they were removed from pharmacists' books. Several herbalists in the sixteenth century made written accounts of the benefits of *Viola tricolor,* including the healing of wounds when applied topically. In his book *Paradisi in sole paradisus terrestris* (1629), botanist John Parkinson refers to the cleansing qualities of the viola, instructing that the flower may be used fresh and green or dried and ground into a powder. Two centuries later, heartsease is described in *Culpeper's Complete Herbal* (1814) as being regularly used in syrup form for treating epilepsy, lung inflammation, and skin conditions as well as for curing syphilis. Through the centuries, it has also be used as a diuretic, tonic, mild laxative, and blood purifier and for the treatment of rheumatism, asthma, pleurisy, and heart disease.

In recent studies that analyzed its chemical composition and evaluated its diuretic properties, *V. tricolor* (*Violae tricoloris herba*) was found to contain high amounts of saponins (6 percent) and mucilages (almost 15 percent). The elevated content of the latter gives the flower anti-inflammatory and palliative properties, which could explain its history for treating lung inflammation, asthma, and bronchitis. It further clarifies why it was used externally for healing wounds and treating skin conditions.

The presence of antioxidant tannins and carotenoids in the viola further support the flower's use in treating heart disease, while small amounts of salicylic acid and salicylates contribute to its role as an antirheumatic. In addition to being made into a syrup, it was often taken as a tea or tonic, using one to two teaspoons of dried flowers or foliage per cup of water.

The pansies and violas we have available today have been hybridized for decades, so determining how effective they are in the modern treatment of these ailments is inconclusive. That's not to say a nice cup of viola tea or some pansy syrup on your morning pancakes doesn't carry any benefit.

Beyond traditional apothecary, pansy essence is used by healers and practitioners of alternative medicine to aid in clearing negative thoughts and healing grief. For those who believe in the spiritual benefits of flowers, pansies are said to open the heart chakra and strengthen the etheric body.

Nineteenth-century viola apothecary jar and syrup bottle

Further Enjoying the Beauty of the Pansy

Pansies and violas are among the most useful flowers in existence. They are prized in the garden, exceptional in vases, delightful in the kitchen, beneficial in health, and inspiring in artwork.

Pressing flowers is an art form all its own, and I don't know that there is any flower more popular or suitable for pressing than the pansy. As my collection of antique garden books grew, I acquired several that included perfectly pressed flowers from the original owners. Finding a flower from over a century prior between the pages of a book is like receiving a gift in the post from a long-distance friend. There are several ways to press flowers. Whether you use the weight of trusty old books or a new flower press made specifically for the task, it is a craft that brings with it boundless joy and possibility.

Pansies also work beautifully in living wreaths. Several years ago, I purchased some frames and tried my hand at them. I started a few different varieties from seed and transplanted them into the prepared frames once they were ready. The loveliest wreaths were the ones that had pansies with large-size blooms and compact growth versus the smaller violas that tended to grow tall and away from the main shape. Because pansies can tolerate cooler temperatures, there is barely a month of the year that I don't have a pansy wreath in bloom. If you have never grown a living wreath, I encourage you to give it a try.

Another way I have come to enjoy my pansies outside the garden, and easily my favorite use aside from filling a vase, is filling my bathtub. Each day, in the cool morning hours, I collect a jarful of pansies and violas to use in my bath that evening. I bought a lovely old apothecary jar from a local antique shop that I use just for this task. I pick the varieties that are most fragrant, because after a few moments in the warm water, their scent is released tenfold and the entire bathroom is permeated with luxurious, delectable fragrance. And if the olfactory enjoyment wasn't enough reason in itself, it is incredibly enchanting to soak in a tub with limitless colors and patterns of pansies floating and swirling around, prompting a night of lovely dreams.

I hope you have found at least a few more ways to open your life and your garden to the possibilities of the pansy and viola. May they ever inspire you with beauty, hope, comfort, remembrance, perseverance, tenacity, and good health.

The Frizzle Sizzle series of pansies are nicely fragrant and one of my favorites to add to the bath.

Resources

Supplies

FOR DURABLE SEED TRAYS AND
HUMIDITY DOMES

Bootstrap Farmer
www.bootstrapfarmer.com

FOR EXCEPTIONAL HANDMADE VASES

Frances Palmer Pottery
www.francespalmerpottery.com

FOR WATERING CANS GUARANTEED
TO LAST A LIFETIME

HAWS
www.haws1886.com

Seeds

Johnny's Selected Seeds
www.johnnyseeds.com

Baker Creek Rare Seeds
www.rareseeds.com

Further Reading

FOR FURTHER STUDY OF THE PANSY
AND VIOLA

Fuller, Rodney. *Pansies, Violas &
Violettas: The Complete Guide.*
Ramsbury, Marlborough, UK: Crowood
Press, 1990.

FOR GROWING AND ARRANGING CUT
FLOWERS

Benzakein, Erin. *Floret Farm's Cut
Flower Garden: Grow, Harvest, and
Arrange Seasonal Blooms.* San Francisco:
Chronicle Books, 2017.
Raven, Sarah. *The Cutting Garden:
Growing and Arranging Garden Flowers.*
London: Frances Lincoln, 1996.

FOR BAKING WITH PANSIES AND EDIBLE
FLOWERS

Stern, Loria. *Eat Your Flowers: A
Cookbook.* New York: William Morrow
Cookbooks, 2023.

FOR PRESSING PANSIES AND OTHER
FLOWERS

Fielding, Amy, and Melissa Richardson.
*The Modern Flower Press: Preserving the
Beauty of Nature.* New York: Harry N.
Abrams, 2022.

Selected Bibliography

Bailey, Liberty Hyde. *The Standard Cyclopedia of Horticulture*. New York: Macmillan, 1935.

Barillet, Jean-Pierre, and Friedrich Lesemann. *Les pensées: Histoire, culture, multiplication, emploi*. Paris: Librairie De La société Botanique De France, 1869.

Brunfels, Otto. *Herbarum vivae eicones*. Strasbourg, Germany: Johann Schott Printers, 1536.

Botanical-Online. 2020 Oct 5. Properties of Pansy.

Cook, Ernest Thomas, ed. *Sweet Violets and Pansies from Mountain and Plain*. London: Country Life; George Newnes, 1903.

Crane, Howard Hamp. *Pansies and Violas for Exhibition and Garden*. London: W. H. & L. Collingridge; New York: Transatlantic Arts, 1951.

Culpeper, Nicholas. *Culpeper's Complete Herbal*. London: Richard Evans, 1814.

Cuthbertson, William. *Pansies, Violas & Violets*. London: T. C. & E. C. Jack, 1910.

Dodoens, Rembert. *Florum et coronariarum odoratarumque nonnullarum herbarum historia*. Antwerp: Christopher Plantin, 1586.

Farrar, Elizabeth. *Pansies, Violas and Sweet Violets*. Berkshire, England: Hurst Village, 1989.

Fuchs, Leonhart. *De historia stirpium commentarii insignes*. Basel: Michael Isingrin, 1542.

Fuller, Rodney. *Pansies, Violas & Violettas: The Complete Guide*. Ramsbury, Marlborough, UK: Crowood Press, 1990.

Genders, Roy. *Pansies, Violas and Violets*. London: Garden Book Club, 1958.

Gerarde, John. *The Herball: or, Generall historie of plantes*. London: Adam Islip, Joice Norton, and Richard Whitakers Printers, 1597.

Harrison, Joseph, ed. *The Floricultural Cabinet and Florist's Magazine*. London: Whittaker, 1841.

Hulme, Frederick Edward. *Familiar Wild Flowers*. London: Cassell, Petter, Galpin, 1883.

Ingram, John. *Flora symbolica; or, The language and sentiment of flowers*. London: Frederick Warne, 1869.

Jekyll, Getrude. *Wood and Garden*. London: Longmans, Green, 1899.

Jordan, Charles, Jack Ballantyne, Jessie Burnie, and William Cuthbertson. *Pansies, Violas and Violets*. London: Macmillan, 1898.

Marcussen, Thomas, Harvey E. Ballard, Jiří Danihelka, Ana R. Flores, Marcela V. Nicola, and John M. Watson. 2022. "A Revised Phylogenetic Classification for *Viola* (Violaceae)" *Plants* 11, no. 17: 2224. doi.org/10.3390/plants11172224

M'Alpine, Daniel. *The Botanical Atlas. A Guide to the Practical Study of Plants Containing Representatives of the Leading Forms of Plant Life*. Vol. I, *Phanerogams*. Edinburgh: W. & A. K. Johnston, 1833.

Parkinson, John. *Paradisi in sole paradisus terrestris*. London: Humfrey Lownes & Robert Young Printers, 1629.

Ruel, Jean. *De natura stirpium libri tres.* Paris: Simon de Colines, 1536.

Rutherford Ely, Helena. *Another Hardy Garden Book.* New York and London: Macmillan, 1905.

—. *A Woman's Hardy Garden.* New York and London: Macmillan, 1903.

Sanders, Thomas William. *The Flower Garden.* London: W.H & L Collingridge, 1907.

Simkins, James. *The Pansy: and How to Grow and Show It.* Birmingham: Cornish Brothers; London: Simpkin, Marshall, 1889.

Sinclair, James, and J. Freeman. *A History and Description of the Different Varieties of the Pansey, or Heartsease, Now in Cultivation in the British Gardens.* London: Effingham Wilson, 1835.

Thomas, Harry Higgott. *The Gardener at Home.* London: Cassell, 1912.

—. *The Ideal Garden.* London: Cassell, 1911.

Toiu, Anca, E. Muntean, Ilioara Oniga, O Voştinaru, and M. Tămaş. Pharmacognostic research on *Viola tricolor* L. (Violaceae). 2009 Jan–Mar. Rev Med Chir Soc Med Nat Iasi; 113(1): 264–267. PMID: 21491816.

Toole, William. *Guide to Pansy Culture and Catalogue of Premium American Pansy Seeds.* Baraboo, Wisconsin: Republic Printers, 1903.

Wittrock, Veit Brecher. "A Contribution to the History of Pansies." *The Gardeners' Chronicle; A Weekly Illustrated Journal of Horticulture and Allied Subjects* 19 (1896): 684, 726–728, 754–755.

Acknowledgments

To Leslie Jonath. My gratitude is immeasurable for your belief in this book and your willingness to take a chance on me. This "little book that could," as you lovingly called it, would not exist without you.

Kelly Bowie, who so dearly captured all my pansies and violas. How lucky I am to work with you on such a heartfelt project and to have had you as my friend for so many decades.

Debbie Berne, your creativity, vision, and honesty were invaluable to this book. Thank you.

Ashley Lima, for stepping in and bringing this book to the finish. Your efforts are so deeply appreciated.

My editing team and everyone at Connected Dots Media, for helping this book become the best version of itself.

Makenna Goodman and Hillary Caudle and the team at Timber Press, for believing in this book and being as excited about sharing it with the world as I am.

Mia Johnson, for turning my initial vision into an extraordinary and beautiful first step.

Susan McLeary, for opening a door for me with such kindness and encouragement. It made all the difference.

The Crowood Press on behalf of Rodney Fuller, I am truly honored by your gracious correspondence and support of this book. Thank you for allowing me to share Mr. Fuller's sketch among its pages.

Erin Benzakein, for pushing me down the pansy rabbit hole with trays full of flowers, packets full of seeds, and a heart full of possibility. I am forever grateful.

For my dearest friends that continuously encouraged, tirelessly supported, and fiercely cheered me on while helping me get this book into print. Renae, Meredith, January, Kate and Nina, thank you for your love and loyalty.

For my mom, whose love and support has always been truly unconditional.

To my boys—the three brothers. Thank you for your support and patience while this book absorbed so much of my attention and time. I am so grateful for your understanding, thoughtfulness, and love.

To my husband, Omar, who believed me capable of things I, myself, questioned. You never hesitate in taking a chance on me. Your support has always been and continues to be unfaltering. Thank you for loving me as you do.

To the many friends, fellow pansy lovers, small business owners, and customers who have supported our little flower farm and the process of creating this book, thank you. I hope my passion and intention have translated adequately within these pages and inspired you to grow more pansies.

Index

pansies
vs. violas, 15–16
Pansies, Violas & Violettas (Fuller), 66
Pansies, Violas and Violets (Genders), 34
Pansies and Violas for Exhibition and Garden (Crane), 33, 70
pansy craze, 18, 28
'Papilio' pansy, 34
Paradisi in sole paradisus terrestris (Parkinson), 225
Parkinson, John, 20, 225
Parr, Katherine, 16
pasta dishes, 222
'Peacock' pansy, 34
pedicels, 68
pensea, 20
pensée, 20
La pensée (Ragonot-Godefroy), 31
Les pensées (Barillet), 31
peony, 205
perennial establishment, 41
'Perfection' viola, 24
pests, 60, 80, 88
pH levels, 48
phlox, 70, 88, 202
phosphate, 47
pink pansies, 24
'Plums and Peaches' pansy, 142
pollinators, 60, 61, 80
Ponsort, Charles Louis, 31
poppies, 202
potassium, 47–48
pots and containers, 60, 69, 70, 93
powdery mildew, 81
pressing flowers, 226
propagation, 75, 77–78
propagaton, 28
'Pumpkin Patch' rose, 214
purplish leaves, 47

rabbits, 88
Ragonot-Godefroy, 31
raised beds, 69
ranunculus, 201
Reed, Mr., 26
Regent's Park, 31
Richardson, Mr., 26
'Rite of Passage' bearded iris, 205
'Rococo' pansy, 145
Roggli family, 33
root division, 78
root rot, 81
root systems, 46, 54
roses, 70, 80, 94, 205, 209, 210, 213, 214, 217
Royal Botanic Society, 31
Ruel, Jean (Ruellius), 20
rust, 82
Rutherford, Helena Ely, 54

salads, 221
Salter, John, 28, 31
saponins, 225
Scottish Pansy Society, 28
Scottish Viola and Pansy Association, 28
seasonal challenges, 86–89
seaweed fertilizer, 47
seedlings, transplanting, 57, 58, 60
seedpods, 72
seeds
collecting, 72
from hybrid varieties, 72
sowing, 51–52, 94
starting, 51–52, 54, 57
storing, 51
self-seeding, 70, 72
shade needs, 39–40, 58
show pansy, 28, 31–32
shrubs, 202
'Silver Edged' pansy, 34
Sinclair, J., 26–27
Slough, Mr., 26

slugs, 60, 80, 83, 85
snails, 60, 83
snapdragons, 202
Société Botanique de France, 31
soil preparation and maintenance, 46–48, 58
Sorbet 'Antique Shades' viola, 170
Sorbet 'Honeybee' viola, 173
Sorbet 'Orchid Rose Beacon' viola, 174
Sorbet 'Phantom' viola, 177
Sorbet 'XP Neptune' viola, 178
Sorbet 'XP Pink Halo' viola, 181
soups, 221–222
spacing, 58
'Spanish Eyes' pansy, 146
Speckle, Veit Rudolph, 20
spider mites, 68, 83
spring flowers, 201–202, 205
spring garden tasks, 43
The Standard Cyclopedia of Horticulture (Bailey), 65
stem length, 68, 69, 70
stock, 202
'Striped' pansy, 34
Stuart, Charles, 24
succession planting, 68
summer flowers, 202, 209, 210, 213
summer garden tasks, 43
sun exposure, 39–40, 58
'Sweet Pea Mix' pansy, 148
sweet peas, 202
sweet violet, 16
Sweet Violets and Pansies, 66
Sweet Violets and Pansies (Cook), 39
Swiss Giants series, 33

Brenna Estrada is an accomplished flower farmer who has built a dedicated following through the sharing of her extensive collection of pansies. Raised in the Pacific Northwest in the shadow of the Cascade Mountains, Estrada spent her childhood hiking mossy trails sheltered by towering pines and abundant flora. This instilled in her a deep love of nature, specifically flowers. After serving five years in the United States Marine Corps and sixteen years as a 911 call taker and police dispatcher, Estrada took a position at Floret Flower Farm, where her knowledge and passion grew, for pansies especially. Every year, she trials around one hundred different varieties of pansies and violas to find those with the most exceptional colors, fragrance, and stem length. Her pansies have drawn the attention of growers and artists from all over the world. She continues to share her passion with others and is working to make seeds from specialty varieties more accessible to both small-scale growers and home gardeners. She currently resides on a lovely little island with her husband and three boys.